CLINTON St. BAKING COMPANY

COOKBOOK

BEER & BURGER
$12, Monday thru Thursday, 6-8pm

CLINTON ST. BAKING
COMPANY
& RESTAURANT

½ Price! All Bo
Monday

LUNCH
Served 11:30 – 4

SERVED ALL DAY

oatmeal — 8.5
With caramelized apples and pears

buttermilk biscuit sandwich — 9
Scrambled eggs, melted cheddar, homemade tomato jam,
with hash browns
with bacon add 2.5

country breakfast — 13
Three eggs any style, grilled 'cure 81' ham steak, hash browns,
buttermilk biscuit

southern breakfast — 14
Two eggs any style, sugar-cured bacon, cheese grits,
fried green tomatoes

spanish scramble — 13
Three eggs, chorizo, tomatoes, caramelized onions, scallions,
melted Monterey Jack, with hash browns and sourdough toast

farmer's plate — 14
Soft scrambled eggs, farmhouse cheese, herb roasted tomatoes,
sourdough toast

brioche french toast — 13
Caramelized bananas, roasted pecans, warm maple butter

pancakes
With Maine blueberry or banana walnut, with warm maple butter

eggs benedict

smoked salmon benedict
With Petrossian smoked sa

huevos rancheros
Sunny side up eggs with red beans
cream, salsa picante, and pepper
add chorizo 2.5

potato pancakes — 12
House applesauce, sour cream

clinton st. omelette — 12
With hash browns and sourdough toast, choice of two: swiss,
cheddar, goat cheese, Monterey jack, muenster, spinach,
chopped tomatoes, mushrooms, bacon, ham, red peppers,
caramelized onions, tomato jam.
Egg whites w greens add 2

beet salad — 9
Soft ripened goat cheese, toasted almonds

spicy shrimp and cheese grits —
Fried green tomatoes, creamy creole sauc

grilled chicken sandwich — 13
Avocado, bacon, chipotle mayo, romaine
on grilled sourdough, with chips and sl

veggie sandwich — 10
Avocado, muenster, beefsteak tomato
mayo on 7 grain toast with mixed gre

po' boy catch of the day — 1
House tartar sauce and romaine on

black angus cheeseburger —
Swiss or cheddar and caramelized
a toasted brioche bun, with chips

russet fries — 4
sweet potato fries — 5

SI

two eggs any style — 4
hash browns — 4
double smoked bacon —
sugar-cured bacon —
pulled turkey —
ham —

CLINTON ST. BAKING COMPANY

COOKBOOK

BREAKFAST, BRUNCH & BEYOND

FROM NEW YORK'S FAVORITE NEIGHBORHOOD RESTAURANT

DEDE LAHMAN & NEIL KLEINBERG

Photography by Michael Harlan Turkell

Ⓛ Ⓑ

LITTLE, BROWN AND COMPANY

New York Boston London

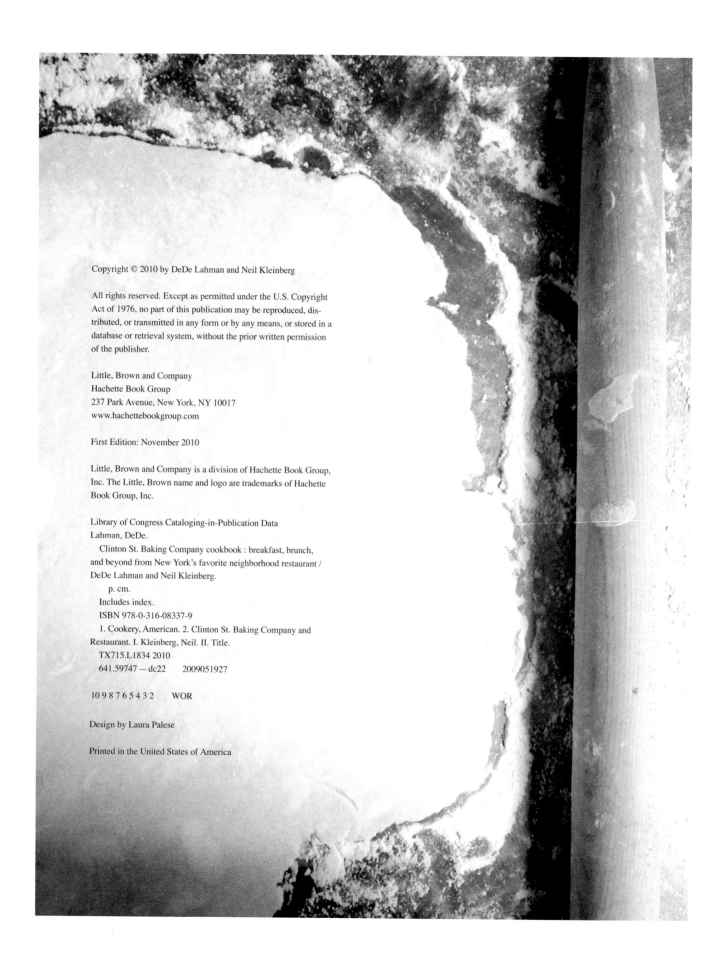

Little, Brown and Company
Hachette Book Group
237 Park Avenue, New York, NY 10017
www.hachettebookgroup.com

First Edition: November 2010

Little, Brown and Company is a division of Hachette Book Group, Inc. The Little, Brown name and logo are trademarks of Hachette Book Group, Inc.

Library of Congress Cataloging-in-Publication Data
Lahman, DeDe.
    Clinton St. Baking Company cookbook : breakfast, brunch, and beyond from New York's favorite neighborhood restaurant / DeDe Lahman and Neil Kleinberg.
        p. cm.
    Includes index.
    ISBN 978-0-316-08337-9
    1. Cookery, American. 2. Clinton St. Baking Company and Restaurant. I. Kleinberg, Neil. II. Title.
    TX715.L1834 2010
    641.59747 — dc22   2009051927

10 9 8 7 6 5 4 3 2   WOR

Design by Laura Palese

Printed in the United States of America

FOR OUR LOVING PARENTS, NANCY AND JERRY LAHMAN
AND THE LATE MILLIE AND JOE KLEINBERG

. CONTENTS .

LOVE & BUTTER
{Introduction} 9

. LOVE & BUTTER .

You might think that a random meeting at a restaurant called A Salt and Battery would be inauspicious for romance, but somehow the fateful night that Neil and I collided at this English fish and chips shop on Greenwich Avenue launched a great affair of love (and butter).

Five minutes of banter, a few laughs, and we were both on our way, separately, out into the cold, wet December night, clutching greasy newspaper-bundled wraps of fried cod, fat chips, and tiny containers of malt vinegar.

Turn your calendar pages ahead just ten months, and there we are, a bit plumper, a lot happier, getting married in a low-ceilinged Greek taverna on Barrow Street in the same West Village. With our relatives, we dance the hora to a Greek-Israeli band in between eating buttery *saganaki* with lemon, sublime *taramasalata,* tender cubes of lamb, and *horiatiki* salad with ripe red tomatoes and rich feta.

Who knew that a few years later we'd own a tiny thirty-two-seat café world famous for its brunch? I was a former magazine editor turned freelance writer turned marketing consultant turned clothing entrepreneur. He was a twenty-five-year veteran of the New York cooking scene on a five-year break, teaching at-risk youth how to run a nonprofit café.

Our restaurant odyssey began, funnily enough, with bad white bread: three squares of store-bought Wonder grilled on the griddle at the Jovial Grill, a French-Chinese restaurant on Clinton Street. It was bamboo-paneled and festooned with the kind of 3-D model ships you'd be more likely to see adorning the walls of an old Howard Johnson's restaurant on Cape Cod than a tiny storefront on the gritty Lower East Side.

"You take this restaurant from me," pleaded Tommy Kong, the owner (now a lawyer), who had once cooked on the line under Neil at the Plaza Hotel's Gauguin restaurant. "You can make this work. You're the only one."

I quietly pretended to nibble on the bread — an appetizer apparently meant to sweeten Tommy's proposition — and considered the prospects. Chinese cook turned personal injury lawyer. Drug-infested street. Undesirable zip code. Ugly decor.

Recipe for disaster, I thought.

"Recipe for success!" Neil said.

We debated. He won (for the last time). And suddenly Neil was baking all night long in his whites, just like a culinary student, high on creamed sugar, French-roast coffee, and blind optimism.

This might not sound like a big deal, but first you need to know that Neil was still working by day at the nonprofit café, teaching culinary arts to those teens. Second, he had no pastry background! His training, at the New York City College of Technology (Hospitality Management) in Brooklyn, was in the French classics: savory food, delicate fish, reduced stocks, rich sauces. That he was able to bake the most delectable muffins from scratch is still astounding to me.

Our mission was simple: to offer the best baked goods in the city, using the freshest ingredients, hand mixed in small batches. And Neil was doing just that. We bought the finest dark French-roast coffee beans, ground them in-house, and hired a college student to serve cappuccino with the warm muffins and scones, mostly to go. Much to our delight, it didn't take long for neighborhood rockers, designers, and business owners to stumble in. We were a true mom-and-pop shop, splitting the labor between us: Neil ran the back of house, and I ran him. (That's what he likes to say.)

Within a few months, the bakeshop's production doubled and wholesale accounts were opened citywide. Even Zabar's and Saks Fifth Avenue's café were selling Neil's baked goods.

Delighted and feeling somewhat legit, we listened closely to what the neighborhood seemed to want. It turned out that they craved soup, and Neil started making as many as five fresh varieties a day — and served them with our signature buttermilk biscuits. They're now a staple of our menu.

That was our gateway to lunch and weekend brunch. Neil went back to his savory roots. Scrambled eggs and cheddar were piled on the buttermilk biscuits, spread with fresh tomato jam. French-style farmers' market omelets and wild Maine blueberry pancakes topped with warm maple butter were added to the menu. And just like that, the craze began. We stood back, wide-eyed, as our tiny weekend crowd grew from 13 a day, to 35, to 60, and now to 340!

What's our secret? Neil says, "It's love." I say it's that we make simple American classics using serious-chef techniques. And then I guess it's also something you can't quite quantify, like a feeling you get at that special favorite joint: that one diner or luncheonette where, on vacation, you bite into the most delicious cheese omelet, crispy-soft waffle, or blueberry muffin made from scratch. Mine was a modular white rectangle of a truck stop next to an old Laundromat in Oakland, Maine, where I worked as a camp counselor. My friends and I didn't even know the restaurant's name, but we'd start every day off there at 10:00 a.m., drinking coffee with real farm cream. Along came perfectly cooked fried eggs and thick house-made toast — dampened with melted butter — that we covered with Smucker's grape jelly from tiny square packets (even those gelatinous purple condiments tasted good).

Neil discovered his life-changing spot in 1975 with cousins, en route from California back home to Brooklyn on a cross-country road trip. It was an old barn in Gunnison, Colorado, with wood paneling and exposed beams where they served little Danish pancakes called *ebelskiver*, filled with apples. Every plate came piled with hash browns, eggs, maple syrup, and grilled ham — the works, with the *ebelskiver* dusted in powdered sugar and plated like the ultimate garnish. Neil still talks about those like an ex-love.

The point is, when you find a favorite joint, where the food hits the spot and you're completely at home — your senses come alive, your belly is full — what more could you want? For the moment, life feels complete.

We're pretty sure this is why on any given Sunday there's a line of people thirty-deep by 9:00 a.m., waiting to get into our little baking company and restaurant. We're still the same unassuming storefront, still just thirty-two seats, and yet people repeatedly travel from Tribeca — and Toronto, and Tokyo — to eat here. What an honor.

Time and time again we've been asked by devoted guests for our recipes, and now, without further ado, here they are. Whether you love pancakes or waffles, bacon or sausage, cake or pie, here's your chance to make our version — explained step by step in Neil's straightforward terms. Just turn the page, whip out your best-quality ingredients, and get ready to learn the secret recipes and methods from inside the Clinton St. bakeshop and kitchen.

1

. BISCUITS .

It all started with the buttermilk biscuit. Anyone worth his or her Brooklyn roots knows that the best biscuits in New York, if not the country, were found at the legendary Lundy's Restaurant in Sheepshead Bay — a.k.a. *the* family seafood destination of the Northern Hemisphere.

With 2,800 seats back in the 1950s and '60s, Lundy's was to Brooklyn what baseball is to America. Lundy's seemed as big as two ball fields to Neil, who, as a kid, made a monthly pilgrimage there on a bus from Flatbush with his entire family because they did not own a car.

Lundy's was most famous for its shore (seafood) dinners, its long, snaking lines (especially on Sunday nights), and, best of all, its flaky buttermilk biscuits. Jamaican waiters dressed in crisp white coats made their way around the tiled-floor dining room each night with hot biscuits piled on plates and wax-paper-wrapped pats of butter sliding around. The minute they hit the table, those biscuits were devoured, with requests for more broadcast across the crowded room (some of the loudest from the Kleinbergs themselves).

When it reopened in 1995, after sixteen years of dormancy, Neil was asked to launch the new Lundy's kitchen as executive chef. It was a dream job, and he could not wait to re-create the restaurant's magic.

His first roadblock came with the recipes, which — he quickly learned — were passed down by its black southern cooks through oral tradition. Not one cup, one ounce, one teaspoon, was recorded on paper. Neil would have to replicate every morsel from memory, beginning with those beloved biscuits. To start, he reconjured their feeling and flavor: small and soft, not too browned on top, fluffy on the inside, slightly crunchy on the outside. The biscuits needed to taste buttery, salty, a touch sugary, and have a starchy quality that held up when a pat of butter slid between two warm halves.

Neil began his research by reading celebrated cookbook writers, everyone from Fannie Farmer to Maida Heatter to Edna Lewis. He tinkered with different flavors, ratios of shortening and butter, regular milk versus buttermilk. Next he tracked down an artisanal flour through the White Lily company in Tennessee, which sold a seminal soft winter wheat.

After weeks of testing, baking, and tasting, he finally found The One, a recipe born of that wonderful flour and a technique of mixing that made those biscuits remarkably flaky and melt-in-your-mouth good. For a child of Brooklyn — a son of Lundy's — it was like reinventing the wheel.

And just like that, one perfect biscuit became eight thousand a day. There were two reach-in refrigerators equipped with pan-slides dedicated solely to the sheet pans with biscuits. Every morning, twenty-five trays on each side of both fridges were filled with punched-out mini biscuits ready to bake.

Naturally, when we opened Clinton St.'s oven doors, Neil's first thought was to serve the biscuits he perfected back at Lundy's. He didn't want to serve bagels or croissants. The biscuit would be the ideal morning staple: the platform on which Neil could rest scrambled eggs, cheddar cheese, his own tomato jam — and, as it turned out, his Brooklyn pride.

BUTTERMILK *Biscuits*

2 CUPS *all-purpose flour,*
plus more for dusting

2 TABLESPOONS *baking powder*

1½ TABLESPOONS *sugar*

¼ TEASPOON *salt*

3 TABLESPOONS *unsalted butter,*
chilled and cubed

3 TABLESPOONS *vegetable shortening,*
chilled and cut into small chunks

¾ CUP *buttermilk*

....

RESTAURANT TRICK *If you have*
a convection oven, bake for 15 to 17
minutes at 325°F. A convection oven
circulates air to bake items such as
cookies, biscuits, and cakes faster and
gives a nicer color to both baked and
roasted items.

COMMON MISTAKE *Do not twist*
the biscuit cutter in the dough. Cut
the biscuits by pushing the cutter
directly into the dough and then lift-
ing the cutter. If you twist the cutter,
the biscuits may not rise.

NOTE *You can make these biscuits*
by hand, without a mixer. Mix the
butter and shortening into the dry
ingredients with your fingertips to
achieve a crumbly texture and use
your hands to combine the buttermilk
into the dough. Make sure to powder
your hands with flour if the dough
gets too sticky.

What to do with that extra buttermilk?
Make our Fried Chicken on page 124,
the Onion Rings on page 129, or But-
termilk Streusel Coffee Cake, page 43.

These biscuits can be prepared and then rested overnight for baking the next day.

1   Preheat the oven to 350°F.

2   Place the 2 cups flour and other dry ingredients in the bowl of an electric mixer. Mix on low speed with the paddle attachment until combined.

3   Add the butter and shortening to the bowl and mix on low speed until the dough reaches a crumbly texture. The butter and shortening should be the size of peas.

4   Turn off the mixer and add the buttermilk to the bowl all at once. Mix very briefly on low speed until the dough just comes together (this should take less than 10 seconds).

5   Turn the dough onto a floured surface and form it into a ball. Lightly knead the dough two or three times until combined.

6   You can bake the biscuits the next day. Dust a sheet pan and the top of the dough with flour and refrigerate, covered with plastic wrap, overnight. Then bring the dough back to room temperature.

7   Pat out the dough to a ¾- to 1-inch thickness. Shape the dough into a rectangle, making the sides high. Using a 2-inch-round biscuit cutter, cut out 4 biscuits. Place them on a sheet pan lined with parchment paper and dust with a sprinkling of flour. Gather the dough scraps and, using your hands, tuck in the bottom of the dough so there are no wrinkles, much like making a bread roll. Form the remaining dough into another rectangle with high sides and cut out 2 more biscuits.

8   Place the pan in the preheated oven for 15 to 17 minutes, or until the biscuits are golden brown and cooked through. Halfway through the baking process, rotate the pan for even browning.

9   Serve warm with butter and our Raspberry Jam (page 160).

BUTTERMILK *Biscuit Sandwiches*

MAKES 2 SANDWICHES

2 *Buttermilk Biscuits (page 17)*

4 TEASPOONS *unsalted butter,*
plus **1 TABLESPOON**

3 *large eggs, whisked together*

¼ **CUP** *shredded cheddar cheese*

4 *bacon* **SLICES,** *cooked, crisp and*
well drained

2 HEAPING TABLESPOONS
Tomato Jam (page 163)

When we first opened Clinton St., Neil wanted a breakfast sandwich made with the biscuit, but it was so big, fluffy, and flaky that he couldn't fix a proper sandwich. Instead he had to make it open-faced. He decided to scramble perfect eggs and lay them on the bottom half with a sprinkling of grated cheddar over the top. On the other half, he couldn't just do ketchup from the bottle, so he decided to make a tomato jam. You can assemble this sandwich with a day-old biscuit because toasting it is what makes it really great anyway. Add two strips of bacon to pull it all together.

1 Preheat your oven's broiler or heat a griddle.

2 Slice each biscuit in half and butter each half with 1 teaspoon butter. Toast the biscuits under the broiler or on a griddle until the butter melts and the biscuit halves are light brown. (Or, instead of toasting the biscuits, you can use a *panini* grill or grill pan to mark the biscuits on the cut side.)

3 In a 9- to 10-inch omelet pan, melt the remaining 1 tablespoon butter. Once the butter is frothy, add the eggs. Gently scramble them in a circular motion with a heatproof spatula, starting from the center of the pan and moving out. Shake the pan to distribute the uncooked eggs. Once the eggs are set, divide them in half in the pan.

4 To assemble the sandwiches, place the eggs on the bottom halves of the biscuits. Place the shredded cheese on top of the eggs. Place the eggs under the broiler to briefly melt the cheese. Crisscross 2 pieces bacon on top of the cheese and dollop the top halves with 1 tablespoon Tomato Jam. Serve with Hash Browns (page 143).

SPANISH *Biscuit Sandwiches*

2 *Buttermilk Biscuits (page 17)*

4 TEASPOONS *unsalted butter,*
plus **1 TABLESPOON**

1 *chorizo sausage, quartered*
vertically

3 *large eggs, whisked together*

¼ CUP *shredded jalapeño Jack cheese*
or Monterey Jack (or 2 slices)

2 HEAPING TABLESPOONS
Tomatillo Sauce (page 165)

This is the biscuit sandwich's Spanish cousin. We split and grill the chorizo to give it that real gutsy charred flavor.

1   Preheat your oven's broiler or heat a griddle.

2   Slice each biscuit in half and butter each half with 1 teaspoon butter. Toast the biscuits under the broiler or on a griddle until the butter melts and the biscuit halves are light brown. (Or, instead of toasting the biscuits, you can also use a *panini* grill or grill pan to mark the biscuits on the cut side.)

3   Grill the chorizo until both sides are crispy and seared. Or you can broil the chorizo in the oven or sauté it in a pan.

4   In a 9- to 10-inch omelet pan, melt the remaining 1 tablespoon butter. Once the butter is frothy, add the eggs. Gently scramble them in a circular motion with a heatproof spatula, starting from the center of the pan and moving out. Shake the pan to distribute the uncooked eggs. Once the eggs are set, divide them in half in the pan.

5   To assemble the sandwiches, place the eggs on the bottom halves of the biscuits. Place the shredded cheese on top of the eggs. Place the eggs under the broiler to briefly melt the cheese. Crisscross 2 pieces chorizo on top of the cheese and dollop the top halves with 1 tablespoon Tomatillo Sauce. Serve with Hash Browns (page 143).

WHOLE WHEAT *Buttermilk Biscuits*

MAKES 6 BISCUITS

1 CUP all-purpose flour, plus more for dusting

1 CUP whole wheat flour

2 TABLESPOONS baking powder

1½ TABLESPOONS sugar

¼ TEASPOON salt

3 TABLESPOONS unsalted butter, chilled and cubed

3 TABLESPOONS vegetable shortening, chilled and cut into small chunks

¾ CUP buttermilk

In 2007 we were opening Community Food & Juice, a more health-conscious restaurant uptown with some of our greatest hits from downtown, and we said, Why not make a whole wheat biscuit? Neil started experimenting with ratios between whole wheat and organic white flour and came up with a nice balance. The biscuits were nutty and grainy from the whole wheat, yet still kept their fluffiness when baked. (Some of our guests like these biscuits better than the original.) Depending on how health-conscious you are, you can use more whole wheat or more white flour in this recipe. Just remember that the more whole wheat flour you use, the darker, more rustic, and less moist and fluffy the biscuits will be. It's a bit of a trade-off.

1   Preheat the oven to 350°F. (See Restaurant Trick, page 17.)

2   Place the 2 cups flour and other dry ingredients in the bowl of an electric mixer. Mix on low speed with the paddle attachment until combined.

3   Add the butter and shortening to the bowl and mix on low speed until the dough reaches a crumbly texture. The butter and shortening should be the size of peas.

4   Turn off the mixer and add the buttermilk to the bowl all at once. Mix very briefly on low speed until the dough just comes together (this should take less than 10 seconds). (See Note, page 17.)

5   Turn the dough onto a floured surface and form it into a ball. Lightly knead the dough two or three times until combined.

6   You can bake the biscuits the next day. Dust a sheet pan and the top of the dough with flour and refrigerate, covered with plastic wrap, overnight. Then bring the dough back to room temperature.

7   Pat out the dough to a ¾- to 1-inch thickness. Shape the dough into a rectangle, making the sides high. Using a 2-inch biscuit cutter, cut out 4 biscuits (see Common Mistake, page 17). Place them on a sheet pan lined with parchment paper and dust with a sprinkling of flour. Gather the dough scraps and, using your hands, tuck in the bottom of the dough so there are no wrinkles, much like making a bread roll. Form the remaining dough into another rectangle with high sides and cut out 2 more biscuits.

8   Place the pan in the preheated oven for 15 to 17 minutes, or until golden brown and cooked through. Halfway through the baking process, rotate the pan for even browning.

9   Serve warm with butter and our house-made Raspberry Jam (page 160).

ST. BAKING
MPANY
RESTAURANT

Cheddar Muffin

CLINTON ST. BAKING
COMPANY
& RESTAURANT
Carrot Raisin Bran Muffin

CLINTON ST. BAKING
COMPANY
& RESTAURANT

Blueberry Muffin

2

MUFFINS & SCONES

{ SWEET & SAVORY }

Even though Neil has been a bagel eater his whole life,
he knew that he couldn't make them in our own bakeshop.
But he did think he could craft muffins and scones as well
as any baker because of their simple method.

He approached recipe development like a savory chef, focusing first on the flavors. He wanted a blueberry muffin actually to taste like berries. He wanted to see pieces of the peach inside the muffin batter. More than anything else, he wanted the base to be like a good cake: very buttery and able to stand up on its own, with the fruit flavor absolutely bursting through.

In the middle of his testing and tasting, we took a quick work trip to Portugal to visit fabric makers for a clothing company I was running at the time. Neil spotted some pastries in very pretty brown-and-gold paper cups and hunted them down when we returned to New York. As he had guessed, these European-style cups were a great vehicle for making muffins and helped them retain their moistness to boot. Plus, he liked that you had to unwrap the cups by hand and thus appreciate their design. It made eating the muffin the greatest simple pleasure.

Perhaps the best thing about these paper cups is that you can bake them at up to 450 degrees and they can withstand the heat; they won't burn. This makes preparation really simple. All you need to do is make your batter, prep your filling, and pour it all into these cups. (These days, it's pretty easy to find silicone muffin pans, which can also withstand up to 450 degrees, and the muffins slide right out.

After achieving somewhat of a cult following for the fruit muffins, Neil decided to try his hand at one that was savory. He took the sweet muffin cake recipe, pulled out the sugar, added salt and pepper, and dreamed up new fillings. The first (and possibly still the best) is the version with bacon and cheddar.

Making muffins is surprisingly easy and a terrific first baking project for any novice because they use what's called a straight dough. Translation: a batter made in stages with the ingredients added straight to the mix. Whatever fillings you choose, make sure they're the best quality you can find. We use natural and organic flavor extracts. You'll see how adding a capful of these extracts to your batch will optimize flavor.

To finish the fruit muffins and make them sing, we add a simple streusel crumb on top. This crumb mix is used not only on top of the muffins but sometimes inside the muffin batter to give it nice texture.

Scones are even easier than muffins. They're like biscuits, only sweeter (and snootier). The less you do to a scone batter, the more tender, crumbly, sweet, and delicious the pastry will come out. Unlike English scones, made sumptuous with Devonshire clotted cream, our scones are a bit more American in style. They're not like tiny cylinders. We free-form them on a baking sheet. And they don't need the clotted cream. They stand up on their own.

. A FEW WORDS .
for Bakers

Here are some great tips and techniques to keep in mind before you make your pastries:

• *Do not overmix the muffin batter.*

• *The best way to get a muffin out of its tin is to use a paper cup as the holder.*

• *When making the batter, frozen fruits are often better because they will actually suspend in the batter and burst open when they bake, infusing the muffin with a lot of flavor. If using fresh fruit, first drain the liquid well.*

• *Use an ice cream scoop or tablespoon for a mess-free way to put your batter into cups or tins.*

• *Scones need an even temperature. Make sure they're cooked through the middle.*

These are the main tools you'll need for baking muffins and scones:

MIXER *(we use a Hobart or KitchenAid) with two attachments: a paddle and a 5-quart bowl.*

RUBBER SPATULA *to scrape down the bowl when adding liquids and solids.*

ICE CREAM SCOOP *with a latch release.*

Good MUFFIN TINS.

BAKING CUPS.

BEST-QUALITY INGREDIENTS *you can find.*

CRUMB MIX

**MAKES 1½ CUPS, ENOUGH
FOR 2 TO 3 BATCHES OF MUFFINS**

½ CUP *all-purpose flour*

½ CUP *sugar*

¼ TEASPOON *cinnamon*

½ STICK (4 TABLESPOONS)
unsalted butter, cubed

....

NOTE *This Crumb Mix has several uses. Try it as a topping for crumb cake, pie, coffee cake, or as a streusel topping. Pulse in a food processor to get the correct consistency. Larger lumps in the crumb mix are okay. You'll just get larger pieces of crumb.*

You've heard of the icing on the cake? This is the equivalent. It's an easy recipe with simple ingredients. Add a bit of cinnamon to it for a nice aroma and flavor. You'll see that the crumb bakes on top and works its way inside as well.

1 Mix the dry ingredients with the butter by hand until the mixture is pea-sized.

2 Keep the Crumb Mix in a cool place until you are ready to use it. The mix can be stored in the fridge for a couple of weeks.

BLUEBERRY *Crumb Muffins*

MAKES 10 STANDARD-SIZED
MUFFINS

½ STICK (4 TABLESPOONS)
unsalted butter, softened

½ CUP *sugar*

½ TEASPOON *vanilla extract*

1 CUP *all-purpose flour*

½ TEASPOON *baking powder*

¼ TEASPOON *baking soda*

1 *large egg*

½ CUP *sour cream*

1 CUP *frozen or fresh blueberries*

10 TABLESPOONS *Crumb Mix
(page 27)*

. . . .

NOTE *If you do not have a standing
mixer handy, use a handheld mixer to
cream the butter, sugar, and vanilla,
then mix the remaining ingredients
together with a spoon.*

Every American bakery seems to have a blueberry muffin. This one's our top seller
and one of our personal favorites.

1 Preheat the oven to 350°F. Lightly grease muffin tins or use paper
muffin cups.

2 In an electric mixer on medium-high speed, with the paddle attachment
cream together the butter, sugar, and vanilla.

3 Sift the remaining dry ingredients together into a bowl.

4 Add the egg to the butter mixture and blend until combined.

5 Add ¼ cup of the sour cream to the butter mixture, then half of the dry
ingredients, mixing and repeating with the remaining sour cream and then the
remaining dry ingredients until the batter is combined. Be sure to end with
the dry ingredients.

6 Fold in the blueberries until evenly mixed.

7 Spoon the batter into the muffin tins, leaving room on the top for the Crumb
Mix. Top each muffin with 1 tablespoon of the Crumb Mix. Bake for 25 to 30
minutes, until a toothpick inserted in the middle of a muffin comes out clean.

8 Cool for at least 10 minutes for best release of the muffins from their tins
(if not using paper liners).

CHERRY *Crumb Muffins*

MAKES 10 STANDARD-SIZED MUFFINS

½ **STICK (4 TABLESPOONS)** *unsalted butter, softened*

½ **CUP** *sugar*

½ **TEASPOON** *vanilla extract*

1 **CUP** *all-purpose flour*

½ **TEASPOON** *baking powder*

¼ **TEASPOON** *baking soda*

1 *large egg*

½ **CUP** *sour cream*

1 **CUP** *frozen or fresh sour pitted cherries (sweet pitted cherries can be substituted)*

10 **TABLESPOONS** *Crumb Mix (page 27)*

....

NOTE *If you do not have a standing mixer, use a handheld mixer to cream the butter, sugar, and vanilla. Then mix in the remaining ingredients with a spoon.*

The best time to make these muffins is in the month of June, when sour cherries are in season. We have a backyard cherry tree in upstate New York, and one summer weekend we found a bear cub clinging to its top branches, eating the cherries and spitting out the pits. Neil had borrowed our neighbor's beautiful antique cherry pitter and had left it under the tree. We never saw it again after that day. You will find that a pitter is helpful when using fresh cherries.

1   Preheat the oven to 350°F. Lightly grease muffin tins or use paper muffin cups.

2   In an electric mixer on medium-high speed, with the paddle attachment cream together the butter, sugar, and vanilla.

3   Sift the remaining dry ingredients together into a bowl.

4   Add the egg to the butter mixture and blend until combined.

5   Add ¼ cup of the sour cream to the butter mixture, then half of the dry ingredients, mixing and repeating with the remaining sour cream and then the remaining dry ingredients until the batter is combined. Be sure to end with the dry ingredients.

6   Reserve 8 cherries and fold in the remaining cherries until evenly mixed.

7   Spoon the batter into the muffin tins, leaving room on the top for the Crumb Mix. Top each muffin with 1 tablespoon of the Crumb Mix and 1 cherry. Bake for 25 to 30 minutes, until a toothpick inserted in the middle of a muffin comes out clean.

8   Cool for at least 10 minutes for best release of the muffins from their tins (if not using paper liners).

Variation

To make Peach Crumb Muffins, substitute 1 cup fresh or frozen sliced peaches for the cherries.

BANANA CHOCOLATE CHUNK *Muffins*

MAKES 10 STANDARD-SIZED MUFFINS

½ STICK (4 TABLESPOONS) *unsalted butter, softened*

½ CUP *sugar*

½ TEASPOON *vanilla extract*

1 CUP *all-purpose flour*

½ TEASPOON *baking powder*

¼ TEASPOON *baking soda*

1 *large egg*

½ CUP *sour cream*

¾ CUP *semisweet chocolate chunks (52–62% cacao; chips can be substituted, or you can make your own chunks from a bar of baking chocolate; see the Note on page 193)*

2 *perfectly ripe to overripe medium-sized bananas, cut into 1-inch chunks*

10 TABLESPOONS *Crumb Mix (page 27)*

....

NOTE *If you do not have a standing mixer, use a handheld mixer to cream the butter, sugar, and vanilla. Then mix the remaining ingredients in with a spoon.*

How can you go wrong with this flavor combination? Toast these muffins and they're like a dessert. Be sure to use really ripe bananas to get an intense banana flavor.

1   Preheat the oven to 350°F. Lightly grease muffin tins or use paper muffin cups.

2   In an electric mixer on medium-high speed, with the paddle attachment cream together the butter, sugar, and vanilla.

3   Sift the remaining dry ingredients together into a bowl.

4   Add the egg to the butter mixture and blend until combined.

5   Add ¼ cup of the sour cream to the butter mixture, then half of the dry ingredients, mixing and repeating with the remaining sour cream and then the remaining dry ingredients until the batter is combined. Be sure to end with the dry ingredients.

6   Fold in the chocolate chunks and bananas until evenly mixed.

7   Spoon the batter into the muffin tins, leaving room on the top for the Crumb Mix. Top each muffin with 1 tablespoon of the Crumb Mix. Bake for 25 to 33 minutes, until a toothpick inserted in the middle of a muffin comes out clean.

8   Cool for at least 10 minutes for best release of the muffins from their tins (if not using paper liners).

RASPBERRY *Yogurt Muffins*

MAKES 8 STANDARD-SIZED
MUFFINS

MUFFINS

½ STICK (4 TABLESPOONS)
unsalted butter, softened

½ CUP *sugar*

¼ TEASPOON *vanilla extract or paste*

1 CUP *all-purpose flour*

½ TEASPOON *baking powder*

¼ TEASPOON *baking soda*

1 *large egg*

½ CUP *plain yogurt*

½ CUP *fresh or frozen raspberries*

2 TABLESPOONS *Raspberry Jam (page 160)*

....

GLAZE

1 TABLESPOON *Raspberry Jam (page 160)*

1 CUP *confectioners' sugar*

NOTE *The base for this recipe is the same as the previous muffin recipes, but we substitute yogurt for sour cream and glaze for our crumb mixture. The yogurt is tangier than sour cream. It doesn't matter which type of yogurt you use, as long as it's plain. Even Greek yogurt works well. If you don't have homemade Raspberry Jam for the glaze, you can substitute raspberry puree, smashed fresh raspberries, or store-bought raspberry jam.*

If you do not have a standing mixer, use a handheld mixer to cream the butter, sugar, and vanilla, then mix the remaining ingredients with a spoon.

The closest we ever get to low-calorie baking is substituting yogurt for sour cream. These muffins happen to be sinfully delicious and remarkably moist. The light frosty glaze on top is adorably pink. It's our daughter Michelle's favorite.

1 Preheat the oven to 350°F. Lightly grease muffin tins or use paper muffin cups.

2 In an electric mixer on medium-high speed, with the paddle attachment cream together the butter, sugar, and vanilla.

3 Sift the remaining dry ingredients together into a bowl.

4 Add the egg to the butter mixture and blend until combined.

5 Add ¼ cup of the yogurt to the butter mixture, then half of the dry ingredients, mixing and repeating with the remaining yogurt and then the remaining dry ingredients until the batter is combined. Be sure to end with the dry ingredients.

6 Fold in the whole raspberries and jam until evenly mixed.

7 Spoon the batter into the muffin tins, filling them to the top. Bake for 25 to 30 minutes, until a toothpick inserted in the middle of a muffin comes out clean.

8 Allow the muffins to cool 10 minutes while you make the glaze. Whisk together the Raspberry Jam with the confectioners' sugar. The glaze will come together in a thick paste. Slowly whisk in 1 tablespoon warm water. The glaze will be the consistency of evaporated milk.

9 Remove the warm muffins from the tins and either dip the muffin tops into the glaze and swirl until the tops are evenly coated or spoon 1 tablespoon of glaze on top and spread evenly.

SUNSHINE *Yogurt Muffins*

MAKES 8 STANDARD-SIZED MUFFINS

MUFFINS

½ STICK (4 TABLESPOONS) *unsalted butter, softened*

½ CUP *sugar*

¼ TEASPOON *vanilla extract*

1 CUP *all-purpose flour*

½ TEASPOON *baking powder*

¼ TEASPOON *baking soda*

1 *large egg*

½ CUP *plain yogurt*

1 TABLESPOON *lemon or lime juice*

1 TABLESPOON *orange juice*

1 TEASPOON *lemon or lime zest*

1 TEASPOON *orange zest*

¼ TEASPOON *lemon extract*

¼ TEASPOON *orange extract*

....

GLAZE

3 TABLESPOONS *lemon, orange, or lime juice (or any combination)*

1 CUP *confectioners' sugar*

....

NOTE *If you do not have a standing mixer handy, use a handheld mixer to cream the butter, sugar, and vanilla, then mix the remaining ingredients together with a spoon.*

This lemon-orange muffin is moist, light, and citrusy-bright. Hence the name, which is silly but apt. It's a big hit at the restaurant and very popular for ladies' teas, showers, and breakfasts — a delicate and delicious splurge. For optimal flavor, use real juice and the best extract you can find.

1   Preheat the oven to 350°F. Lightly grease muffin tins or use paper muffin cups.

2   In an electric mixer on medium-high speed, with the paddle attachment cream together the butter, sugar, and vanilla.

3   Sift the remaining dry ingredients together into a bowl.

4   Add the egg to the butter mixture and blend until combined.

5   Add ¼ cup of the yogurt to the butter mixture, then half of the dry ingredients, mixing and repeating with the remaining yogurt and the remaining dry ingredients until the batter is combined. Be sure to end with the dry ingredients.

6   Mix in the citrus juices, zests, and extracts until combined.

7   Spoon the batter into the muffin tins, filling them to the top. Bake for 25 to 30 minutes, until a toothpick inserted in the middle of a muffin comes out clean.

8   Allow the muffins to cool 10 minutes while you make the glaze. Whisk together the juice with the confectioners' sugar. The glaze will come together in a thick paste and then loosen as the citrus breaks down the sugar. The glaze will be the consistency of evaporated milk.

9   Remove the warm muffins from the tins and either dip the muffin tops into the glaze and swirl until the top is evenly coated or spoon 1 tablespoon of glaze on top and spread evenly.

APPLE RAISIN *Bran Muffins*

MAKES 8 STANDARD-SIZED MUFFINS

1 ¼ **CUPS** *bran flakes*

2 ½ *medium apples*

1 ⅛ **CUPS** *all-purpose flour*

1 **TEASPOON** *baking soda*

½ **TEASPOON** *salt*

¾ **CUP** *light brown sugar*

1 *large egg*

1 **CUP** *buttermilk*

½ **CUP** *canola or vegetable oil*

¾ **CUP** *golden or dark raisins*

....

NOTE *Bran flakes can be found in a health food store or specialty baked goods store.*

This recipe comes from Andrea Rappaport, a great chef in San Francisco and Neil's cousin-in-law. When Neil first opened the bakery, she gave him inspiration with a few of her best recipes.

1   Preheat the oven to 350°F. Lightly grease muffin tins or use paper muffin cups.

2   Put the bran flakes in a small bowl and pour in ½ cup hot water. Mix. The bran will absorb the water and become fluffy.

3   Peel, core, and grate (with the largest side of a box grater) 2 of the apples. Slice and reserve the remaining apple half, skin on, for the topping.

4   Place all of the dry ingredients in a large bowl and whisk until incorporated.

5   Add the egg, buttermilk, and oil and mix until all the ingredients are combined. Scrape down the sides of the bowl. Add the bran, grated apples, and raisins and fold them into the batter.

6   Use a ⅓ cup measure to scoop the batter into muffin tins.

7   Top each muffin by pushing a reserved apple slice onto each muffin.

8   Bake for 12 to 15 minutes, until the muffins are golden brown.

SCONES

MAKES 6 LARGE SCONES

2 CUPS *all-purpose flour, plus more for dusting*

¼ CUP *granulated sugar*

½ TEASPOON *salt*

1 TABLESPOON *baking powder*

1 CUP *heavy cream*

3 TEASPOONS *turbinado sugar*

Many scone recipes contain milk and butter, but we use heavy cream, which is a combination of the two. Cream pulls the whole recipe together and makes the scones flaky and irresistible. When you take this spoon batter out of the mixer and pour it on a pan to bake, it will be fluffy like a biscuit and subtly sweet.

1 Preheat the oven to 350°F.

2 Combine the 2 cups flour and the next three dry ingredients in the bowl of a mixer with the paddle attachment, using the low-speed setting (or mix by hand).

3 Stop the mixer and add the heavy cream to the dry ingredients. Mix on low speed until the dough has combined (less than 10 seconds).

4 Dust your counter with flour and dump out the scone mixture. Pat the dough into a circle, about ¾ to 1 inch thick. Cut the dough into 6 even triangles. Roughly form each triangle into a round shape. Place the round scones on a parchment-paper-lined sheet pan (or use nonstick cooking spray).

5 Top each scone with ½ teaspoon turbinado sugar. Bake for 18 to 20 minutes, until golden brown and baked all the way through. Rotate the pan halfway through for even browning.

Variations

GOAT CHEESE AND HERB *Add ½ cup crumbled goat cheese and ½ cup chopped fresh herbs (chives, parsley, thyme, rosemary, or any combination thereof) with the heavy cream to the dry scone ingredients. Omit the turbinado sugar.*

MIXED BERRY *Add ½ cup frozen blueberries and ½ cup frozen cranberries (use fresh if the berries are in season) to the dry ingredients in the mixing bowl. It's easy to use frozen berries with this mix because the flour coats them and helps to distribute them evenly. When you add the cream, be sure not to overmix. The berries should remain partially frozen. Do not let the berries defrost before incorporating them.*

CHOCOLATE CHUNK *Add 1 cup chocolate chunks (see the Note on page 193) to the dry ingredients in the mixing bowl.*

SAVORY *Goat Cheese & Herb Muffins*

MAKES 12 LARGE MUFFINS

2½ CUPS *all-purpose flour*

3 TABLESPOONS *sugar*

1 TABLESPOON *salt*

1 TABLESPOON *baking powder*

1 TEASPOON *baking soda*

1 TEASPOON *ground white pepper*

4 TABLESPOONS *mixed chopped herbs, such as parsley, chives, thyme, rosemary (fresh makes all the difference)*

1¾ CUPS *half-and-half*

2 *large eggs*

½ CUP *unsalted butter, melted*

½ CUP *crumbled goat cheese*

Savory muffins are a unique twist on an old classic, and they always surprise people. Why didn't I think of that? is a common reaction after tasting one for the first time. The greatest thing about these muffins is that they stay incredibly light and moist yet make a very hearty snack. When paired with a delicious soup (try our Tomato Zucchini Bisque, page 101), you've got a fabulous little meal!

1   Preheat oven to 375°F (or 325°F if using a convection oven). Lightly grease muffin tins or use paper muffin cups.

2   Measure and sift all the dry ingredients into a large mixing bowl. Stir mixed herbs into the dry ingredients to evenly distribute the herbs, ensuring that they will be in every bite of muffin.

3   In a medium mixing bowl, whisk together 1¼ cups of the half-and-half with the eggs and melted butter. Mix until combined well.

4   Add the dry mix to the wet mix with a spoon or whisk. Stir to combine, but do not overmix. Once combined, add the remaining half-and-half. Fold in the goat cheese, using a rubber spatula. There should be specks and pieces of goat cheese throughout the batter. Pour the batter into the muffin tins and bake 22 to 24 minutes, until golden brown on top and a toothpick inserted into the middle of a muffin comes out clean.

5   Allow the muffins to cool 10 minutes and serve warm.

BUTTERMILK STREUSEL *Coffee Cake*

MAKES ONE 10-INCH BUNDT CAKE

STREUSEL TOPPING

¾ CUP *light brown sugar*

½ CUP *all-purpose flour*

¼ CUP *rolled oats*

½ CUP *chopped walnuts*

¼ CUP *granulated sugar*

¼ CUP *graham-cracker crumbs*

4 TABLESPOONS *unsalted butter, melted*

1 TEASPOON *ground cinnamon*

¼ TEASPOON *ground nutmeg*

....

CAKE

2 STICKS (16 TABLESPOONS) *unsalted butter, softened*

2 CUPS *sugar*

4 *large eggs*

2 CUPS *buttermilk*

2 TEASPOONS *vanilla extract*

2 TEASPOONS *coffee extract or freshly brewed espresso (or strong coffee)*

4½ CUPS *all-purpose flour*

1 TEASPOON *baking powder*

1 TEASPOON *baking soda*

½ TEASPOON *salt*

This very easy recipe yields a surprisingly beautiful cake with a dense, buttery texture. The unique streusel "topping" actually becomes the bottom when the cake is inverted, and the height of this cake and the gorgeous arch of the streusel inside make it look professionally made. Bake this one for your mother-in-law.

1   Preheat the oven to 300°F. Grease and flour a 10-inch Bundt or tube pan.

2   Mix all the Streusel Topping ingredients together in a mixing bowl with a wooden spoon. Set aside.

3   For the cake, cream together the butter and sugar. Add the eggs two at a time, mixing until well blended.

4   Mix in the buttermilk and extracts.

5   Sift together and stir in the remaining dry ingredients.

6   Fill the pan halfway with the batter. Sprinkle with two-thirds of the Streusel Topping. Add rest of the batter. Top with remaining one-third streusel.

7   Bake for 60 to 70 minutes, until a toothpick inserted in the middle comes out clean.

8   Cool. To unmold, place a plate firmly on top of the pan and flip, being careful to preserve the streusel.

LEMON-LAVENDER *Loaf Cakes*

MAKES FOUR 3-BY-5-INCH LOAVES

CAKE

2 STICKS (16 TABLESPOONS) *unsalted butter, softened*

1½ CUPS *sugar*

3 *large eggs*

2½ CUPS *all-purpose flour*

1 TABLESPOON *baking powder*

¼ TEASPOON *salt*

¾ CUP *whole milk*

1 TEASPOON *vanilla extract*

2 TEASPOONS *lemon extract or lemon oil*

1 TEASPOON *lemon zest*

2 TABLESPOONS *freshly squeezed lemon juice*

....

GLAZE

1 CUP *superfine or granulated sugar*

4 TABLESPOONS *freshly squeezed lemon juice*

1 TEASPOON *lemon extract or lemon oil*

1 TEASPOON *dried lavender buds*

....

NOTE *If you do not like lavender, simply leave it out for delicious lemon loaves.*

We love serving this delicious cake to our catering clients, particularly those hosting ladies' occasions like baby showers and bridal breakfasts. Edible lavender is not easy to find (try your gourmet grocer or health food store), but it adds a special touch that perfectly complements the zesty lemon flavor in these loaves. It is crucial to use fresh-squeezed lemon juice. Organic lemons are best because their rinds are especially fragrant when grated.

1 Preheat the oven to 350°F. Grease and flour four 3-by-5-inch loaf pans.

2 For the cake, cream together the butter and sugar in a standing mixer on medium speed until light and fluffy, approximately 5 minutes.

3 Add the eggs one at a time, mixing well in between so that each is fully incorporated.

4 Sift together the remaining dry ingredients into a bowl.

5 Mix the milk, extracts, and zest in a separate bowl.

6 Add the dry and wet ingredients alternately, mixing and repeating until the batter is combined, ending with the dry ingredients.

7 Add lemon juice. Do not overmix.

8 Pour the batter into the prepared loaf pans.

9 Bake for 35 to 40 minutes, until golden on top.

10 Mix all the glaze ingredients together in a bowl until the sugar is dissolved. Pour into a shallow bowl or plate.

11 When the cakes are baked (a toothpick inserted in the middle comes out clean), let them cool in their pans for 5 minutes. While still warm, unmold them and roll in the glaze on all sides, including the top. Put the cakes back in the molds (this can be tricky — try placing the pans over each cake before flipping them) until they fully cool. Unmold again and serve.

JALAPEÑO *Cornbread*

**MAKES EIGHT MUFFINS OR SIX
3-BY-5-INCH MINI LOAVES**

1 ⅔ CUPS *whole milk*

1 STICK (8 TABLESPOONS) *unsalted butter, melted*

2 *large eggs*

1 ⅔ CUPS *all-purpose flour*

1 ⅓ CUPS *cornmeal*

¾ CUP *sugar*

3 TABLESPOONS *cornstarch*

1 TABLESPOON *baking powder*

1 ½ TEASPOONS *salt*

½ TEASPOON *ground white pepper*

1 ½ TABLESPOONS *minced fresh jalapeño pepper, seeds removed*

....

TRY THIS *Wear latex or kitchen gloves while handling the jalapeño to avoid the burn.*

Jalapeño Cornbread is perfect with our Buttermilk Fried Chicken (page 124), Pulled Pork & Eggs (page 61), or just plain with a big pat of butter. We love the way the fiery jalapeño complements the light sweetness of the corn flavor. It's a rockin' combination.

To make regular cornbread, simply omit the jalapeño from the recipe.

1 Preheat the oven to 350°F. Grease and flour 8 muffin tins or 6 mini loaf pans.

2 Whisk all the wet ingredients together in a bowl.

3 Mix all the dry ingredients in another bowl with the jalapeño.

4 Mix the wet and dry ingredients together with a whisk or spoon in a larger bowl. Do not overmix.

5 Pour the batter into the tins or loaf pans.

6 Bake for 20 minutes or until a toothpick inserted into the center of a muffin or a loaf comes out clean.

3

EGGS, EGGS, EGGS

It's 1977. Neil has just graduated New York Tech's culinary school, and he's thrilled to land his first job as a cook at the twenty-four-hour Empire Diner on 23rd and Tenth. On his inaugural day, Jon Simon — Neil's best friend, fellow grad, and already an Empire chef — tells him to crack sixty dozen eggs into two five-gallon buckets for brunch.

With all the seriousness and care of a surgeon, Neil cracks those eggs one by one, then carries the buckets downstairs to the walk-in fridge, but he's so nervous, so excited, so energized, that he knocks over one of the buckets. Yolks and whites everywhere. Needless to say, he had some cleaning to do. Now, over thirty years later, Neil's own kitchen goes through hundreds of dozens of eggs a week, and each cage-free, organic egg is cracked by Hugo Sanchez, our fastidious prep cook, who has been with us for six years. He's manned the same station day in, day out: like a Zen master squeezing fresh juice, making tartar sauce, and separating eggs for Neil's perfect, beautiful, lemony hollandaise.

· FLIP & TUCK ·

The Perfect Omelet

The secret to making the perfect omelet is knowing when to flip it onto the plate. Your eggs are set, your filling is hot, and you tuck it in like a baby in a blanket. Neil perfected his French-style omelets in Cooking 101 at New York Tech in Brooklyn. His favorite teacher, Professor Panzarino, hosted many an intimidating Omelet Day, where Neil and his classmates lined up in a row down a long, hot stovetop, shaking their pans in a hurry, just as if they were in a restaurant kitchen. The eggs had to be made quickly — whisk the yolks and whites, agitate the pan (not the chef), stir. This was an Olympic workout.

When creating an omelet at home, the first mistake many cooks make is to let the eggs sit too long in the pan. The second mistake is flipping the omelet over and cooking both sides. *Non, non, non.* When creating a classic three-fold French omelet, cook the eggs on only one side. The key is to leave the top slightly creamy and undercooked, so that when your ingredients are added, and the omelet is flipped and tucked, the inside stays soft, fluffy, and melted.

FRENCH-STYLE *Omelet*

MAKES 1 OMELET

3 *eggs any size, preferably cage-free organic*

Salt and ground black pepper

1 TABLESPOON *unsalted butter*

Any combination of fillings, such as grated Swiss, cheddar, goat cheese, Monterey Jack, or Muenster; spinach; chopped tomatoes; mushrooms; bacon or ham; roasted red peppers; caramelized onions, or Tomato Jam (page 163)

....

TRY THIS *When you start the flip, hold the handle of the pan and place the pan edge in the middle of the plate. Shake gently so that when you roll the omelet onto the plate, you'll have the leverage and the ability to fix a mistake in case you didn't do it just right.*

RESTAURANT TRICK *In restaurants the omelet gets heated from above in a salamander oven (a small broiler) for thirty seconds to a minute before the flip to warm the filling and make any cheese melt. At home, a hot oven or open broiler will do nicely, but keep in mind: your goal is to warm the inside, not the top.*

1   Crack the eggs into a bowl. Add a pinch of salt and pepper to taste. Whisk the eggs with a fork to break them up and mix them thoroughly until they look like foamy orange juice. You shouldn't be able to see pieces of white or pieces of yolk.

2   Heat an omelet or fry pan over a medium flame until it's hot. Add the butter, swirl it around until it's melted but not browned, foamy but not burned. If the butter browns too fast, your pan is too hot.

3   Pour or ladle your eggs into the pan. You'll know the pan is hot enough because the eggs will start curling up around the edges.

4   Agitate the pan a bit and move the eggs with a spatula as though you're giving them a light scramble, until they're a little bit creamy and a little bit fluffy, 1 to 2 minutes. The entire bottom of the pan should be covered. Turn off the heat and add your fillings.

5   Time for the flip and tuck — picture rolling down the side of a hill, arms tight by your side, and you've got the right idea. (a) First flip over one end of the omelet with your hand or a spatula to partly cover the filling; (b) next, with your hand or a spatula, gently roll the omelet over again. (c) Nudge it onto the plate with a spatula or your other hand. When the omelet is out of the pan, form the omelet on the plate with your hand, literally tucking in the sides to make a beautiful, oval, plump little packet. (d) The top of the omelet will look fluffy and blond, without any browning, with both ends of the omelet hidden underneath and the "seam" on the bottom of the plate.

SOUTHERN *Breakfast*

SERVES 2

8 SLICES *Sugar-Cured Bacon*
(page 148)

4 TEASPOONS *unsalted butter*

4 *large eggs*

PINCH *of salt*

PINCH *of ground white pepper*

1 CUP *Creamy Cheese Grits*
(page 130)

4 *Fried Green Tomatoes (page 132)*

Fresh parsley or chives, minced

....

NOTE *This breakfast is delicious
with poached, fried, or scrambled
eggs, but we like them over easy.*

HELPFUL HINT *Assemble all of
the ingredients in advance — before
you begin cooking the eggs.*

This dish is a perfect balance of the senses. It is our favorite breakfast on the menu. Finished with cheddar and Monterey Jack cheese, the white grits are a creamy, savory, delicious base. The juicy, crisp bricks of tomatoes act as toast for the eggs, and the grits sop up the rest. The caramelization of the bacon adds a special sweet note. This perfect southern breakfast is great with a little green or red Tabasco on the side, or our Tomatillo Sauce (page 165).

1   Preheat the oven to 350°F.

2   Reheat the Sugar-Cured Bacon in the oven for 5 minutes to recrisp the slices.

3   Warm 2 teaspoons of the butter in an omelet pan or nonstick pan over medium heat until the butter is foamy. Carefully crack 2 eggs into a bowl, making sure there are no shells and that the yolks are intact. Season the eggs with a pinch of salt and pepper. Pour the eggs into the pan. Once the eggs are set (this will take about 30 to 40 seconds), gently move the pan from side to side in order to loosen them. Tilt the pan downward and jerk your wrist in an upward motion toward yourself in order to flip the eggs over. Make sure to flip the eggs when they are loose in the middle so that the egg whites protect the yolks. Allow them to cook for 15 seconds and flip the eggs back. Remove the eggs from the pan and keep them warm. Cook the remaining 2 eggs using the same method.

4   To assemble each plate, spoon ½ cup grits onto a warm plate and set 2 Fried Green Tomatoes off to the side. Place 2 eggs on each plate on the other side of the grits and crisscross 4 slices bacon on top in the center. Garnish the plate with parsley or chives and serve with hot sauce on the side.

Huevos Rancheros

SERVES 2

½ CUP *Mexican Red Beans
(page 135)*

TWO *10-inch flour tortillas*

¼ CUP *jalapeño Jack or Monterey
Jack cheese, shredded*

1 TO 2 *medium plum tomatoes,
roughly chopped*

½ *small red onion, thinly sliced*

1 TABLESPOON *fresh cilantro,
chopped*

1 TABLESPOON *canola oil or clarified
butter (see page 143)*

4 *large eggs*

PINCH *of salt and ground
black pepper*

½ CUP *Guacamole (page 154)*

¼ CUP *Jalapeño Sour Cream
(page 156)*

....

NOTE *For easy assembly, make sure
all of your ingredients are handy and
prepared.*

*You can also use chorizo in this
recipe. Slice 1 chorizo into rounds and
pan-fry in 1 teaspoon oil until crispy
and browned. Use a slotted spoon to
remove the chorizo from the pan and
drain well. Add to other toppings.*

This is a bright and beautiful homage to many on our great kitchen staff who originally came from Puebla, Mexico. All of the components of this dish are very special, from the Guacamole to the way we cook our red beans, from the Jalapeño Sour Cream to the organic farm-fresh eggs. It has become a classic. Some of our guests like to wrap up the Huevos like a burrito and take a big bite, which is ingenious and minimizes their work with a knife and fork. Others like to pick it apart and save their favorite ingredients for last. Either way, it's an entire meal and then some.

1   Preheat the oven to 350°F.

2   Warm up the beans in a skillet or saucepan over low heat.

3   Sprinkle each tortilla with 2 tablespoons cheese and heat on a grill, griddle, or in a 10-inch nonstick sauté pan (cheese side up) until the cheese starts to melt and the bottom of the tortilla is lightly browned. The tortilla will start to bubble on the sides.

4   While the tortilla is warming, combine the chopped tomatoes, sliced onion, and chopped cilantro to make a rustic salsa.

5   Heat the oil in a 10-inch oven-safe skillet over medium-high heat. Carefully crack 2 eggs into a bowl, making sure there are no shells and that the yolks are intact. Season the eggs with a pinch of salt and pepper. Pour the eggs into the pan and fry them until the outsides are crispy and the whites are set. Place the pan and eggs into the oven in order to cook the eggs on top till the white parts are no longer clear. Repeat with the remaining 2 eggs.

6   To serve, top each tortilla with 2 eggs. On top of the eggs, place 2 tablespoons warmed beans, 2 tablespoons of the rustic salsa mixture, ¼ cup Guacamole, and 2 tablespoons Jalapeño Sour Cream. Serve open-faced.

EGGS *Benedict*

SERVES 2

Hollandaise Sauce (recipe follows)

2 TABLESPOONS *salt, plus a pinch*

2 TABLESPOONS *distilled white vinegar*

2 *Buttermilk Biscuits (page 17)*

4 TEASPOONS *unsalted butter*

½ TEASPOON *canola oil*

TWO ¼-INCH-THICK SLICES *smoked ham*

PINCH *of ground white pepper*

4 *large eggs*

1 *plum tomato, chopped*

2 *scallions, chopped (white and green parts)*

. STEPS TO THE .

Perfect Benedict

The steps to the perfect Benedict are quite involved, but the prep order is best as follows:

1 *Make the hollandaise*

2 *Perfectly poach an egg*

3 *Toast the biscuit (or base)*

4 *Grill the ham (or meat)*

The key to eggs Benedict is hollandaise sauce, which pulls the whole dish together. Without a really good homemade hollandaise, eggs Benedict, quite frankly, stinks. Hollandaise is all about time and temperature, and it can be tricky. Like Goldilocks's porridge, hollandaise can't be too cold, or too hot. It has to be just right.

Hollandaise is an egg sauce derived from one of the seven mother sauces in classical French cuisine. It should be light and frothy like chiffon, lemony, well seasoned, and the color of a newly ripe banana. It should run over the eggs gracefully and not stick on top or coagulate. For its flavor, you want to taste butter first, then yolk.

Most often, eggs Benedict is served on an English muffin, which is perfectly serviceable, but we serve ours on a biscuit, split it in half, slathered with butter, and toasted so that it gets very crunchy on the top side and stays nice and moist in the middle. Once assembled, it crumbles on the fork, it's both sweet and savory, and it works beautifully with ham or smoked salmon.

1 Preheat the oven's broiler.

2 Make the hollandaise.

3 Fill a 6-quart saucepan three-quarters full with water. Add the 2 tablespoons salt and vinegar to the water and bring it to a lively simmer over medium heat.

4 Split the biscuits in half and spread each side with 1 teaspoon butter. Toast the biscuits under the broiler until golden brown and the butter is melted.

5 Spread the oil on the ham and season it with a pinch of salt and pepper. Grill the ham until it is marked and then cut each slice in half.

6 Crack 1 egg into a small bowl. Imagine that the pot is a clock and make sure the handle is at 9:00. Starting at 12:00, drop the egg carefully into the simmering water. Drop the next egg in at 1:00, then 2:00, and so on. This way you will know in which order to remove the eggs from the water. The eggs should be removed with a slotted spoon when they are still jiggly but the yolks are set, after about 1½ to 2 minutes.

7 To assemble the Benedict, place 1 half slice ham on top of a biscuit half. The poached egg will be placed on top of the ham. Ladle 1 to 2 tablespoons hollandaise on the egg and then scatter the chopped tomato and a sprinkling of scallions on top.

HOLLANDAISE *Sauce*

MAKES 4 TO 6 SERVINGS

2 STICKS (16 TABLESPOONS) *unsalted butter*

3 *large egg yolks*

2 TEASPOONS *freshly squeezed lemon juice*

PINCH *of cayenne pepper*

½ TEASPOON *salt*

PINCH *of ground white pepper*

....

RESTAURANT TRICKS

The salt and vinegar gives flavor to the poached eggs and keeps them together as well. If the eggs do not come out of the simmering water looking perfect, you can always use a knife to neaten them up.

If you ever "break" a hollandaise (if the sauce gets too hot or too cold and separates), whisk the hollandaise into a tablespoon of hot water to bring it back. It's really about temperature.

TIPS FOR PERFECT HOLLANDAISE

Use the shell of the egg to help you separate the yolks from the whites into bowls, or crack the entire egg into a bowl and fish out the yolk with a spoon. You can use the egg whites to make an omelet.

The stainless-steel or glass bowl should fit comfortably on top of the saucepan of simmering water. Make sure that the bottom of the bowl does not touch the water.

Neil judges the merit of all breakfast places on the strength of their hollandaise alone. He says if there's good hollandaise, he knows there's a real chef in the kitchen.

1   Over medium-low heat, melt the butter. Once it is melted, set the butter aside in a warm place.

2   Fill a saucepan three-quarters full with water and bring it to a simmer over medium heat.

3   In a medium-sized stainless-steel or glass bowl, whisk the yolks with the lemon juice and seasonings until combined. Whisk in 2 tablespoons room-temperature water.

4   Place the bowl on top of the simmering water and continue to whisk the yolks while turning the bowl clockwise. Use a pot holder or kitchen towel because the bowl will get warm! Keep the heat to a minimum so you don't curdle the eggs.

5   After 1 minute, the yolks will become foamy and loose. After 2 minutes, the foamy texture will begin to subside and the yolks will thicken slightly. Make sure to whisk around the sides of the bowl so that the yolks do not congeal. (If they appear to be thickening too quickly or clumping, remove the bowl from the pan and let them cool down.) After 3 minutes of continuous whisking, the eggs will be even thicker and creamy. (Take a break here if you need it. Remove the bowl from the heat, then resume.) At this stage, the yolks are close to being cooked. After 4 minutes, the egg mixture will thicken into ribbons and you will be able to see the bottom of the bowl. Whisk continuously. You will reach the final stage after 5 minutes, when the yolks will be a thick and golden yellow, similar to the texture of mayonnaise. Remove the bowl from the pan.

6   Add the warm melted butter in a steady stream into the yolks, whisking the entire time. The sauce will begin to emulsify after about 1 minute. Keep the sauce on a warm water bath or on the back of the stove and covered with plastic wrap so that a skin does not form on the surface. This hollandaise will keep for 3 to 4 hours. If it becomes too thick, whisk in more room-temperature water.

CRAB CAKES *Benedict*

MAKES 4 SERVINGS

Hollandaise Sauce (page opposite)

5 *large eggs*

¾ CUP *fresh white breadcrumbs*

¼ CUP *mayonnaise, such as Hellmann's or Best Foods*

1 TABLESPOON *freshly squeezed lemon juice*

1 TABLESPOON *chopped fresh parsley*

1 TABLESPOON *chopped capers*

1 TABLESPOON *minced white onion*

1 TEASPOON *Dijon mustard*

1 TEASPOON *plus* **2 TABLESPOONS** *salt*

¼ TEASPOON *ground white pepper*

PINCH *of cayenne pepper*

1 POUND *lump crabmeat*

4 TEASPOONS *canola oil*

2 TABLESPOONS *white distilled vinegar*

12 SPEARS *asparagus, steamed*

This is a great New Year's Day brunch dish because the crab cakes are rich and absorb a lot of the alcohol from the night before. It's also a good Benedict recipe option because the crab cakes serve as the bread. Shellfish always signifies something a little extra special. Pull this one out anytime you have guests.

1   Preheat the oven to 350°F.

2   Make the Hollandaise Sauce.

3   In a large bowl, mix together 1 beaten egg, ½ cup breadcrumbs, the mayonnaise, lemon juice, parsley, capers, onion, mustard, 1 teaspoon salt, and both peppers. Fold in the crabmeat and shape eight 3-by-1-inch-high cakes with your hands. Dredge the cakes in the remaining ¼ cup breadcrumbs.

4   In a sauté pan, heat 2 teaspoons of the canola oil until shimmering over medium-high heat. Sauté 4 crab cakes in the pan, flipping after 2 minutes. The crab cakes will be golden brown and crisp. Allow them to cook 2 more minutes and place on a sheet pan. Repeat the process with the remaining crab cakes. Place the pan in the oven and bake for 3 to 4 minutes, until the crab cakes are cooked all the way through the center.

5   While the crab cakes are baking, crack one egg at a time into a small bowl.

6   Fill a 6-quart saucepan three-quarters full with water. Add the remaining 2 tablespoons salt and the vinegar to the water and bring it to a lively simmer over medium heat.

7   Imagine that the saucepan is a clock and make sure the handle is at 9:00. Starting at 12:00, drop 1 egg carefully into the simmering water. Drop the next egg in at 1:00, then 2:00, and so on. This way you will know in which order to remove the eggs from the water. The eggs should be removed with a slotted spoon when they are still jiggly but the yolks are set, after about 1½ to 2 minutes.

8   To assemble, place 2 warm crab cakes on a plate and top each cake with a well-drained poached egg and top with hollandaise. Serve with asparagus on the side.

SMOKED *Salmon Benedict*

MAKES 2 SERVINGS

Hollandaise Sauce (page 58)

2 TABLESPOONS *salt*

2 TABLESPOONS *distilled white vinegar*

2 *Buttermilk Biscuits (page 17)*

4 TEASPOONS *unsalted butter*

4 *large eggs*

4 *large slices smoked salmon, Nova or Scottish*

2 TABLESPOONS *minced fresh chives*

....

RESTAURANT TRICK *The salt and vinegar gives flavor to the poached eggs and keeps them together as well. If the eggs do not come out of the simmering water looking perfect, you can always use a knife to neaten them up.*

NOTE *The smoked salmon should have a silky texture and should not be overly salty.*

Using the best-quality smoked salmon raises the level of this dish. Either a hand-sliced Nova Scotia salmon, a Scottish variety, or an Irish salmon will do quite well. At the restaurant, we use smoked salmon from Petrossian, a specialty company that deals in caviar, smoked fish, and other delicacies.

1 Preheat the oven's broiler.

2 Make the Hollandaise Sauce.

3 Fill a 6-quart saucepan three-quarters full with water. Add the salt and vinegar to the water and bring it to a lively simmer over medium heat.

4 Split the biscuits in half and spread each side with 1 teaspoon butter. Toast the biscuits under the broiler until golden brown and the butter is melted.

5 Crack 1 egg into a small bowl. Imagine that the saucepan is a clock and make sure the handle is at 9:00. Starting at 12:00, drop the egg carefully into the simmering water. Drop the next egg in at 1:00, then 2:00, and so on. This way you will know in which order to remove the eggs from the water. The eggs should be removed with a slotted spoon when they are still jiggly but the yolks are set, after about 1½ to 2 minutes.

6 To assemble the Benedict, place 1 slice of smoked salmon on top of a biscuit half. Place a poached egg on top of the salmon. Ladle 1 to 2 tablespoons hollandaise on the egg and then scatter the chives on top.

PULLED *Pork & Eggs*

SERVES 4

1 POUND *pulled pork or roasted pork butt, pulled into shreds, juices reserved*

2 TEASPOONS *plus* **2 TABLESPOONS** *salt*

¼ TEASPOON *ground white pepper*

2 TABLESPOONS *distilled white vinegar*

8 *large eggs*

Jalapeño Cornbread (page 45)

2 TABLESPOONS *unsalted butter*

2 TABLESPOONS *chopped fresh cilantro*

Tomatillo Sauce (page 165)

If you make barbecued pulled pork, use the leftover meat for this breakfast dish the next day.

1   Preheat the oven to 350°F.

2   Warm the pulled pork with all reserved juices, 2 teaspoons salt, and the pepper in a sauté pan over medium-high heat. The juices will become a creamy gravy, which will keep the pork moist.

3   Fill a 6-quart saucepan three-quarters full with water. Add the remaining 2 tablespoons salt and the vinegar to the water and bring it to a lively simmer over medium heat.

4   Crack 1 egg into a small bowl. Imagine that the saucepan is a clock and make sure the handle is at 9:00. Starting at 12:00, drop the egg carefully into the simmering water. Drop the next egg in at 1:00, then 2:00, and so on. This way you will know in which order to remove the eggs from the water. The eggs should be removed with a slotted spoon when they are still jiggly but the yolks are set, about 1½ to 2 minutes.

5   While the eggs are poaching, cut 4 slices of cornbread. Butter and toast them in the oven until crisp and the butter is melted.

6   To assemble, place a quarter of the pulled pork in the center of each plate, making sure to include some of the gravy. Place 2 poached eggs on top and sprinkle with ½ tablespoon of the chopped cilantro. Serve with a cornbread slice and Tomatillo Sauce on the side.

SPANISH *Scramble*

SERVES 4

8 *large eggs*

1 TEASPOON *salt*

¼ TEASPOON *ground white pepper*

2 *chorizo links (or andouille or any spicy southwestern sausage)*

1 TABLESPOON *unsalted butter*

½ CUP *Caramelized Onions (page 114)*

½ CUP *plum tomatoes, chopped*

½ CUP *scallions, minced (white and green parts)*

½ CUP *Monterey Jack cheese, shredded*

½ CUP *chopped fresh parsley or chives*

....

NOTE *If you have leftover sausage, try our Andouille Sausage Gumbo on page 102.*

This is the bakery's top-selling egg dish of all time. What makes it so great is that it has everything you could want in an omelet — but it's in a massive scramble, with melted cheese on top. It's the most comforting, satisfying, straight-ahead dish on the planet, and we make it extra special with chorizo — something most everyone likes but few keep every day in their fridge.

1   Preheat your oven's broiler.

2   Whisk the eggs with salt and pepper together in a bowl until combined.

3   Trim the ends off the chorizo and slice the links into ¼-inch rounds. In an oven-safe sauté pan or skillet, heat the butter over medium-high heat until foamy and melted. Sauté the chorizo rounds until they become light brown. Add the onions, tomatoes, and scallions to the pan. Gently sauté the ingredients so they are evenly dispersed.

4   Lower the heat and add the eggs. Move the pan from side to side so that a crust forms on the edge, similar to creating an open-faced omelet. After 1 minute, the eggs will begin to set. Sprinkle the cheese on top and place the pan under the broiler until the cheese has melted.

5   Cut the eggs into quarters in the pan and use a spatula to place each quarter on a plate. Sprinkle the scramble with parsley or chives and serve with Hash Browns (page 143).

SMOKED SALMON *Scramble*

SERVES 4

4 SLICES *seven-grain bread*

8 *large eggs*

PINCH *of ground white pepper*

2 TABLESPOONS *unsalted butter*

8 SLICES (8 OUNCES) *smoked salmon, Nova or Scottish*

6 TABLESPOONS *cream cheese, softened*

½ CUP *minced scallions (green and white parts)*

½ CUP *minced fresh chives*

....

NOTE *Do not use whipped cream cheese for this recipe. We prefer Philadelphia Cream Cheese.*

You can chop the salmon into bite-sized pieces before adding it to the pan.

This is our sophisticated take on lox, eggs, and onions. It's easy to make and goes well with seven-grain toast or a toasted bagel and butter on the side. Better yet, scoop up the scramble onto pieces of your toast and eat it like an eighty-year-old Jewish man. Salad greens lightly dressed with lemon juice and extra virgin olive oil or with a mild vinaigrette make the perfect lunch accompaniment.

1   Toast the bread, according to preference.

2   Whisk together the eggs and white pepper in a bowl until combined.

3   In a 9- to 10-inch omelet pan, melt the butter over medium heat. Once the butter is frothy, add the eggs. Gently scramble them in a circular motion with a heatproof spatula, starting from the center of the pan and moving outward. Shake the pan to distribute the uncooked eggs. Once the eggs begin to set, add the salmon, breaking it up with your spatula and distributing it throughout the egg mixture. Add the cream cheese, 1 tablespoon at a time. Continue to lightly scramble the eggs so that the ingredients are evenly distributed. Add the scallions and remove the eggs from the heat.

4   For each plate, serve the eggs with a slice of toast, sliced again on the diagonal. Sprinkle chives on top of the eggs (salt seasoning is not necessary because the salmon is salty).

FRITTATA

SERVES 1

3 TABLESPOONS *extra virgin olive oil or clarified butter (see page 143)*

HALF *a medium zucchini cut into 1-inch cubes*

2 TABLESPOONS *chopped white onion*

HALF *red or yellow bell pepper, cut into 1-inch cubes*

1 CLOVE *garlic, smashed, peeled, and chopped*

4 TO 6 LEAVES *fresh basil, coarsely chopped*

Salt

Ground white pepper

3 *large eggs*

3 TABLESPOONS *soft or crumbly goat cheese (avoid aged or hard)*

1 TEASPOON *chopped fresh parsley or chives*

It's fun to serve this dish in the cast-iron pan in which it's cooked, giving it a rustic look and feel. The flavor is fresh, and with its healthful profile (nothing breaded or super-sauced), this is a top seller on the weekends for those who don't want the bread, potatoes, bacon, or biscuit that comes with most of our other egg dishes. You can make this frittata with egg whites, but ensure that they don't stick by using a very hot, well-greased pan. You can add anything you want, but this recipe is a good starting point. A spoon of Tomato Jam (page 163) interspersed with the goat cheese dollops will give you a beautiful, creamy, colorful frittata.

1   Preheat the oven to 350°F.

2   Heat a medium-sized sauté pan over a high flame for a minute.

3   Add 1½ tablespoons olive oil or clarified butter.

4   Add zucchini, onion, pepper, and garlic and sauté for 3 to 4 minutes, until cooked and lightly caramelized.

5   Add basil, sprinkle with salt and pepper, and set aside.

6   Whisk together the eggs with salt and pepper in a small bowl until combined. Heat an oven-safe 6-inch cast-iron skillet or 6- to 7-inch nonstick pan over medium heat until 1 tablespoon olive oil or clarified butter thinly coats the pan and sides and is rippling. Add the eggs to the pan. (The eggs should curl up on the sides.) With a heat-safe spatula, continuously move the cooked eggs to the center so that the runny eggs will continue to cook. This method will form a nice crust.

7   When the eggs begin to set, add the vegetable mix, distributing the ingredients across the surface of the frittata. Add the goat cheese by the tablespoon, evenly dotting the frittata.

8   Bake for 7 to 8 minutes in the oven, until the eggs have set and the goat cheese is melted. Scatter the chopped herbs across the top and drizzle with the remaining ½ tablespoon olive oil. Serve warm, either in the pan or on a dish. If not serving from the pan, let the frittata rest for 4 to 5 minutes before attempting to transfer it.

TRUFFLE *Fried Eggs*

SERVES 4

½ CUP *bacon lardons, tightly packed*

4 TO 6 *sprigs fresh thyme*

½ CUP *wild mushrooms (king oyster, shiitake, or field), cut into large chunks*

½ CUP *artichoke hearts, fresh or frozen*

1 CUP *haricots verts or* 1 *bunch asparagus*

2 TABLESPOONS *Truffle Vinaigrette (recipe follows)*

1 TABLESPOON *canola oil, or more if needed*

8 *large eggs*

¼ TEASPOON *salt*

PINCH *of ground white pepper*

½ CUP *minced fresh chives*

Extra virgin olive oil

....

RESTAURANT TRICK *Lardons are chopped slices of thick-cut bacon. You can usually find these ready-made in grocery stores — but if not, make your own: ask your butcher for a piece off of a slab of unsliced bacon, then cut vertically into ½-inch slices and cut the slices horizontally into thirds.*

This is a very savory dish that also works well for celebrations and special events, given its premium ingredients. These days truffle oil is overused (we don't like cooking with it as much as we like using it in a vinaigrette), but you can't deny its seductive powers. Serve this with some beautiful soft butter lettuces, and you have a very elegant meal, suitable for breakfast or dinner.

1   Preheat the oven to 350°F.

2   In a sauté pan over medium heat, sauté the lardons with the thyme until the lardons are crispy and golden. Add the mushrooms and artichokes to the bacon fat and sauté them until tender and brown. As the mushrooms and artichokes are sautéing, trim and blanch the haricots verts or asparagus spears.

3   Remove and discard the thyme sprigs. Add the haricots verts or asparagus to the pan and sauté them until they are warmed through. Add the Truffle Vinaigrette and stir until everything is evenly coated with the dressing. Turn the heat to low and continue to keep the vegetables warm.

4   Heat the canola oil in a 10-inch oven-safe skillet over medium-high heat. Carefully crack 2 eggs into a bowl, making sure there are no shells and that the yolks are intact. Season the eggs with the salt and pepper. Pour the eggs into the pan and fry them until the outsides are crispy and the whites are set. Transfer the eggs from the pan onto a plate and reserve. Add more canola oil to the pan, if necessary, and repeat with the remaining eggs. Once all the eggs are fried, return them to the warm skillet and put the skillet into the oven in order to cook the eggs on top, so the white parts are no longer clear.

5   To assemble, place the vegetables in the center of each of 4 plates, topping with 2 fried eggs. Sprinkle the eggs with minced chives and drizzle them lightly with olive oil.

NOTE *The dressing will stay fresh for 1 to 2 months, stored in the fridge.*

Serve the Truffle Fried Eggs with any green and seasonal vegetables. If you do not have fresh or frozen artichoke hearts, you can substitute canned artichokes packed in water (not oil marinade) or use a whole medium artichoke heart, pared into wedges. Artichoke bottoms would also work in this recipe.

Truffle Vinaigrette

MAKES 2 CUPS

¼ **CUP** *chopped black truffle peelings in liquid*

¼ **CUP** *sherry or red wine vinegar*

1 *shallot, finely minced*

2 **TEASPOONS** *fresh thyme leaves (stems discarded)*

1 *small clove garlic, minced*

1 **CUP** *canola or grapeseed oil*

½ **CUP** *truffle oil*

Mix together the truffle peelings, vinegar, shallot, thyme leaves, and garlic with a whisk in a bowl until combined. Slowly add the canola or grapeseed oil to the mixture in a steady stream, whisking continuously until combined and well emulsified. Repeat with the truffle oil.

FARMER'S *Plate*

SERVES 1

3 *large eggs*

2 TABLESPOONS *heavy cream*

Salt

Freshly ground white pepper

1 TABLESPOON *unsalted butter*

2 TABLESPOONS *extra virgin olive oil*

2 *plum tomatoes, cut in half lengthwise*

¼ CUP *fresh whole basil leaves*

2 SLICES *sourdough toast or baguette*

THREE ¼-INCH-THICK SLICES *farmhouse cheddar cheese*

Fresh chives, minced

This dish is inspired by a layover we had at Gatwick airport on the way home from Tuscany via London. It was 7:00 a.m., and we were starved, cold, and tired. Neil foraged the food stalls for something edible and returned with a steaming plate decorated with perfectly scrambled eggs, roasted vibrant red tomatoes, and a wedge of thick country cheddar. It looked so good that I was convinced it was a trick. Sure enough, it was one of the most remarkable meals of the trip. The next summer, Neil replicated the dish at our cabin rental on a lake in Maine. He embellished it with local farm-stand basil, and a star was born.

1   Preheat the oven to 350°F.

2   Whisk together the eggs with the cream in a bowl until combined. Season the eggs with salt and pepper.

3   In a 9- to 10-inch omelet pan, melt the butter over low heat. Once the butter is frothy, add the eggs. Gently scramble them in a circular motion with a heatproof spatula, starting from the center of the pan and moving outward. Shake the pan to distribute the uncooked eggs. Once the eggs begin to set, remove them from the heat and keep them warm. They should be soft and creamy.

4   In a separate oven-safe sauté pan, heat 1 tablespoon of the olive oil until hot. Add 3 tomato halves (reserving 1 half for another use) skin side down. Sprinkle with salt and pepper and add the basil to the pan. Pour the remaining tablespoon olive oil over the top of the tomatoes. Allow to cook for 30 seconds and flip. Turn the tomatoes back over after 30 more seconds and place the pan in the oven. The tomatoes are ready when they have become juicy and soft and the basil has crisped.

5   Serve the eggs in the middle of a plate with the tomatoes and cheese on one side and the toast or baguette on the other. Sprinkle with chives.

4

. PANCAKES .

....

Most diners use a premade mix for their pancakes
and stir in milk and a couple of eggs for the greatest of ease.
Slapped on the griddle, these pancakes flatten, get tough, and
absorb a slightly burnt taste from the overused grill.

....

Add insult to injury with a heavy dousing of fake maple syrup (90 percent corn syrup and artificial flavors), and you get a dumbed-down flavor experience and a postbreakfast sugar high — and crash. When we first started serving breakfast at the bakery, Neil wanted classically authentic pancakes on the menu — something delicious, wholesome, truly satisfying, and as natural as could be. He looked through old recipes and decided to make two flavors: blueberry, studded with lots of tiny wild Maine berries, and banana-walnut, topped with fresh sliced bananas and toasted walnut pieces for a crunchy, rich mouthful. After a few weeks of experimentation, he came up with an incredibly textured pancake base that was fluffy, chewy, and crispy on the edges, with all the complexity of a yeast-risen cake.

The addition of his luscious, toffeelike, warm Maple Butter made these pancakes the ultimate indulgence and, eventually, the thing for which people wait around the block. We serve five hundred orders of pancakes a week: not bad for a small thirty-two-seat joint.

NEIL'S *Pancakes*

MAKES EIGHTEEN TO TWENTY 3-INCH PANCAKES

4 CUPS *all-purpose flour*

1 TABLESPOON *baking powder, plus* **1 TEASPOON**

¾ CUP *sugar*

1 TEASPOON *salt*

6 *large eggs, separated*

3 CUPS *whole milk*

¾ CUP (12 TABLESPOONS) *unsalted butter, melted, plus* **2 TEASPOONS** *unmelted for the griddle*

1 TEASPOON *vanilla extract*

2½ CUPS *blueberries or sliced bananas and* **1 CUP** *chopped walnuts*

½ CUP *confectioners' sugar or cinnamon sugar for dusting*

Maple Butter (recipe follows, page 78)

....

COMMON MISTAKE *Many cooks don't heat the griddle enough, which is why the first pancake is usually a dud. Make sure it's very hot, then put the butter on. A teaspoon or tablespoon is fine. Use just enough so that the pancake doesn't stick.*

NOTE *To ensure that the whites whip up to maximum height, clean and dry all of your utensils. Also, when separating, be careful not to get any yolk into the whites.*

NOTE ABOUT PEAKS *Peaks are "soft" when you put your finger in the whites and they fall over. Peaks are "medium" when you put your finger in and they drip over a bit and stand up. "Stiff" peaks develop when you whip the whites longer and they stay up.*

Here's the secret of our pancakes: we fold egg whites into the batter. Neil discovered early on in the bakery's existence that if he applied his French techniques — that is, you make a cake lighter by folding in whites (almost like a soufflé) — the batter gets lighter but retains the springy resiliency that makes for a proper pancake. The other key to magnificent pancakes is to avoid overmixing, which creates gluten in the flour and makes them tough.

1   Measure and sift all the dry ingredients into a large (preferably stainless-steel) mixing bowl: flour, baking powder, sugar, salt.

2   In another bowl, whisk together the yolks, milk, melted butter, and vanilla until combined. Whisk the wet mixture into the dry mixture. The result should be slightly lumpy, yet combined to form a batter.

3   Whip the egg whites in a medium mixing bowl until they reach medium peaks (soft in the middle). You can either whip them by hand with a whisk, or put them in the bowl of an electric mixer to whip. Be careful, you don't want to overwhip the egg whites.

4   Gently mix half of the whipped whites into the batter with a large rubber spatula. Then gently fold the remaining half into the batter. Remember: this batter should be slightly lumpy and have large parts of egg whites not fully incorporated; it should look like whitecaps in the ocean with foam on top. (The batter will last a few hours in the fridge without deflating too much.)

5   Heat a griddle — either an electric griddle, a stovetop griddle, or a big flat pan — to 350 to 375°F. Grease the hot griddle with the remaining butter. Drop ¼ cup (approximately 4 tablespoons) of pancake batter on the griddle and cook to set. Add 1 tablespoon blueberries or sliced bananas and 1 teaspoon walnuts before turning the pancakes. Never add the fruit to the mix; always add the fruit to the pancakes once they're on the griddle. When you see bubbles start to form on top, lift the pancake halfway up to see if it's golden brown and crispy on the edges. If ready, flip the pancake.

6   When the pancake is golden brown on both sides, remove with a spatula. Repeat with the remaining batter and filling, cooking several pancakes at a time. Garnish with confectioners' sugar for the blueberry pancakes, cinnamon sugar for the banana-walnut. Serve warm with Maple Butter.

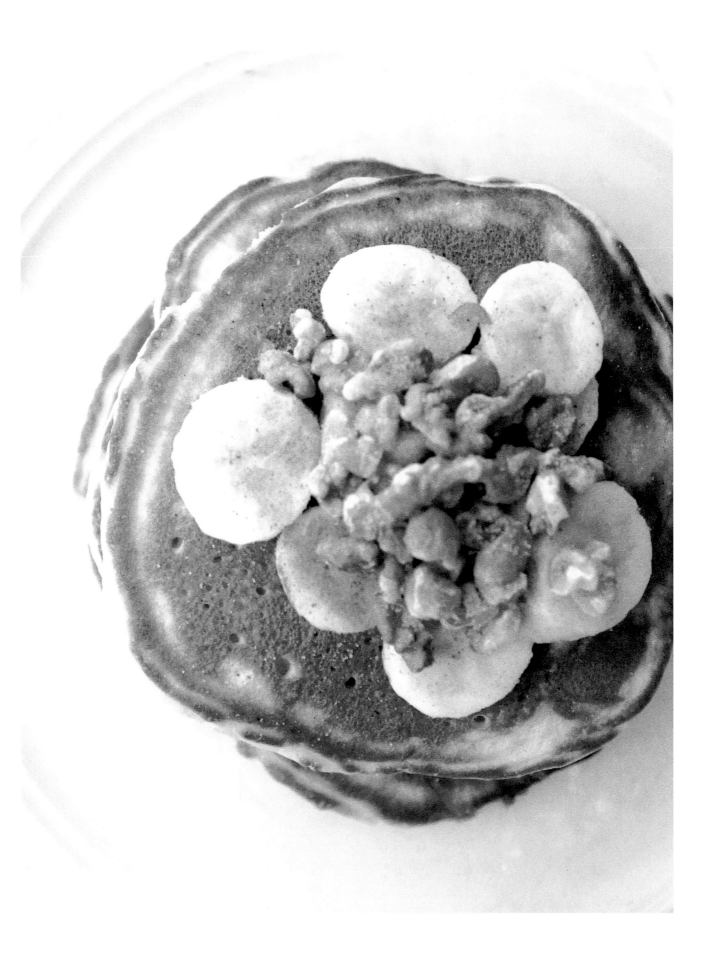

MAPLE *Butter*

MAKES 2 CUPS

1 CUP *real maple syrup*
(we prefer grade-B organic)

2 STICKS (16 TABLESPOONS)
cold unsalted butter, cut into cubes

One Monday morning in winter, we were going through the guest register that we leave out at the host stand during weekend brunch, and here's what we saw scrawled in huge red block lettering: "I WANT TO WIPE THAT MAPLE BUTTER ALL OVER MY BODY!"

'Nuff said.

We make this Maple Butter in four-gallon batches, going through eight gallons per weekend. It's easy, but you absolutely have to make it with real maple syrup.

Nothing dresses your pancakes, French toast, or waffles quite like real maple syrup. The common practice when approaching a huge stack is to put pats of butter in between your pancakes and then pour maple syrup over it, combining the best of both worlds. This was the inspiration for our Maple Butter.

Take maple syrup, warm it up on the stove, and then whisk in pieces of cold sweet butter. You're essentially making a *beurre blanc* sauce (using the classic French technique of whisking something cold into something hot to create an emulsification).

1 Heat the maple syrup over medium heat.

2 Add the cold butter to the warm syrup by whisking in a few cubes at a time until the sauce is smooth and all of the butter is incorporated.

3 Turn off the flame and keep the sauce in a warm place until ready to serve. It will keep for at least two months in the refrigerator. Never boil the syrup.

PANCAKE MONTH

Every February we launch our official pancake month, where we serve a different special pancake daily. We got the idea because February tends to be a slow month, and we wanted to energize our staff, kitchen, and dining room. We printed postcards with the corresponding flavors and days and hoped people would come. The first year it was definitely busier than usual. People seemed happy with new flavors like crunchy pecan with warm maple caramel and fresh blackberries with passion fruit curd. The second year, guests were even more enthusiastic, coming in especially for the new lineup. By the third year, a frenzy had broken out, with people calling, trying to reserve, and even (a few confessed) taking time off from work to taste the candied blood orange and chocolate or strawberries and champagne zabaglione. What's the most popular topping? Year after year: caramelized pineapple, roasted macadamia nuts, and toasted coconut (page 84).

SPECIAL *Pancake Toppings*

MAKES 6 SERVINGS

½ CUP *semisweet chocolate chunks (52–62% cacao; see the Note on page 193)*

Confectioners' sugar for dusting

Hot Fudge Sauce (page 179)

Chocolate Sauce

12 OUNCES *bittersweet chocolate, chopped*

1 CUP *light corn syrup*

½ CUP *half-and-half*

1 OUNCE *unsalted butter*

1 TEASPOON *vanilla extract*

1 TEASPOON *ground chili powder*

1 TEASPOON *ground cinnamon*

....

Crunchy Bananas

1 CUP *flour*

½ CUP *cornstarch*

1 TABLESPOON *baking powder*

½ TEASPOON *ground cinnamon*

¼ TEASPOON *salt*

1½ CUPS *seltzer water or club soda*

Canola or peanut oil

4 *bananas, peeled and halved horizontally*

Cinnamon sugar (2 tablespoons sugar and ¼ teaspoon ground cinnamon)

Classic Chocolate Chunk

1   Stud the pancakes with the chocolate chunks before flipping or top each stack with a scattering of chunks.

2   Dust with confectioners' sugar and serve Hot Fudge Sauce on the side.

Crunchy Bananas with Cinnamon Chili Chocolate Sauce

1   Melt the chocolate, corn syrup, half-and-half, butter, vanilla, chili powder, and cinnamon together in a stainless-steel bowl over a pot filled with warm water on low heat. Mix until smooth. Keep warm until ready to serve.

2   In a large bowl, mix together the flour, cornstarch, baking powder, cinnamon, and salt with a whisk. Continue whisking as you slowly pour in the seltzer. Set aside.

3   Fill a Dutch oven halfway with oil. Heat the oil to 350°F, checking the temperature with a candy thermometer. Roll the banana halves in the batter and place them on a dish. With tongs, dip a banana tip into the oil and hold firm until the oil begins to bubble. Gently drop the banana half into the oil. Fry 2 banana halves at a time for 2 to 3 minutes, or until the bananas turn golden brown and crisp. Use a slotted spoon or skimmer to agitate the bananas every 30 seconds so they do not burn on one side. Repeat with the remaining bananas.

4   Place the fried bananas on a paper-towel-lined plate. Slice the bananas on the bias into 1-inch pieces and sprinkle them with cinnamon sugar. Serve the slices on top of the pancakes with the Cinnamon Chili Chocolate Sauce.

½ CUP *freshly squeezed lemon juice*

¾ CUP *sugar*

1 STICK (8 TABLESPOONS) *unsalted butter*

4 *large eggs*

2 CUPS *heavy cream*

3 CUPS *fresh raspberries*

Zest of 1 lemon

Raspberry Caramel Sauce (page 178)

Fresh Raspberries & Whipped Lemon Cream

1 Make lemon curd by melting together the lemon juice, sugar, and butter in a metal or glass bowl over a pan of simmering water. In a separate bowl, whisk together the eggs. Add the eggs to the lemon mixture and whisk continuously for 10 to 15 minutes. Briefly take the bowl off of the double boiler every 5 minutes to scrape down the sides and prevent curdling. Once the mixture has thickened, cool and whisk occasionally.

2 Whip the heavy cream with a handheld mixer or by hand to create whipped cream with medium-stiff peaks. Gently fold in the cooled lemon curd until the whipped cream becomes a pale yellow color.

3 To assemble, top each individual stack of pancakes with 3 heaping tablespoons whipped lemon cream and top with fresh raspberries and lemon zest. Serve Raspberry Caramel Sauce on the side.

2 CUPS *Burgundy or sour cherries, pitted (canned, dried, or frozen)*

Semisweet dark chocolate curls or shavings (we prefer Callebaut), from an 8-ounce bar

Confectioners' sugar for dusting

....

NOTE *Use Valrhona, Scharffen Berger, or Ghirardelli chocolate if you cannot find Callebaut.*

RESTAURANT TRICK
To make chocolate curls, peel the edges of a thick bar of chocolate with a vegetable peeler. To make shavings, use a heavy 8- or 10-inch chef's knife to rock back and forth across a thick bar of chocolate.

Burgundy Cherries & Chocolate Shavings

1 Strain the cherries if they are packed in juice and reserve the juice. If using dried cherries, reconstitute them in a bowl of hot water for 15 minutes, then drain, reserving the liquid. Reduce the cherry juice or liquid by half over medium heat in a saucepan to make a glaze.

2 When the liquid is syrupy, add the cherries and cook them for 2 to 3 minutes, until the mixture comes together like a sauce.

3 You can stud some of the pancakes with the cherries before flipping to give the pancakes more flavor and texture. Or stack each individual serving of warm pancakes and top with 2 tablespoons of the cherry sauce and thick chocolate curls or shavings. Dust with confectioners' sugar.

3 *large Granny Smith apples (or any other tart variety)*

3 *large pears (Bartlett, Anjou, or Bosc)*

JUICE *of half a lemon*

PINCH *of salt*

2 PINCHES *of cinnamon*

2 TABLESPOONS *unsalted butter, melted*

¼ CUP *sugar*

Almond Praline Brittle (page 176)

Cinnamon sugar (2 tablespoons sugar and ¼ teaspoon cinnamon)

Caramelized Apples & Pears with Praline & Cinnamon

1   Preheat the oven to 375°F.

2   Peel and core the apples and pears. Cut each half into quarters. You should have 48 pieces. Mix the fruit in a bowl with the lemon juice, salt, and a pinch of the cinnamon. Mix in the melted butter.

3   Spread the fruit on a cookie sheet in one even layer and roast in the oven for 15 to 20 minutes until the fruit is caramelized but not burned.

4   Remove the fruit from the oven and sprinkle the surface with the sugar and an additional pinch of cinnamon. Roast until the sugar has caramelized on top of the fruit and a sauce has begun to form, about 8 to 10 minutes.

5   You can stud some of the pancakes with the apple and pear mixture before flipping to give the pancakes more flavor and texture. Or you can stack each individual serving of warm pancakes and top with 1 tablespoon of the apples and pears and crumbled praline. Dust with cinnamon sugar.

1½ CUPS *macadamia nuts, toasted*

1 TABLESPOON *unsalted butter*

2 TABLESPOONS *light brown sugar*

2 CUPS *fresh pineapple, cut into 1-inch cubes (core removed)*

½ TEASPOON *vanilla extract*

1 CUP *white unsweetened flaked coconut*

....

NOTE   *Pecan halves or pieces can be substituted for the macadamia nuts. The coconut can be left plain or toasted, according to preference.*

Caramelized Pineapple, Macadamia Nuts, & Toasted Coconut

1   With an 8- or 10-inch chef's knife, coarsely chop the nuts and reserve.

2   In a 9-inch sauté pan over high heat, lightly brown the butter. Once it is past the foaming stage, add the sugar and cook until melted. Use a spoon to break up any sugar lumps. Add the pineapple chunks and mix in until coated. Add the vanilla extract. Cook until the pineapple becomes caramelized and golden brown, but not mushy and overcooked. Be careful to keep the pan steady so that the chunks will caramelize.

3   You can stud some of the pancakes with macadamia nuts and the caramelized pineapple before flipping to give the pancakes more flavor and texture. Or you can stack each individual serving of warm pancakes and top with 2 tablespoons of the caramelized pineapple and 1 tablespoon of macadamia nuts. Sprinkle with coconut flakes.

FRENCH *Toast*

3 *large eggs*

1½ CUPS *half-and-half*

¼ CUP *granulated sugar*

1 TEASPOON *cinnamon*

1 TEASPOON *vanilla extract*

¼ TEASPOON *lemon extract*

¼ TEASPOON *orange extract*

6 TO 8 SLICES (1-INCH THICK) *brioche or challah bread*

5 TABLESPOONS *unsalted butter*

⅓ CUP *light brown sugar*

2 *medium-ripe bananas, cut into 1-inch slices on the bias*

2 TABLESPOONS *cinnamon sugar (2 tablespoons sugar and ¼ tablespoon cinnamon), plus more for sprinkling*

Toasted pecan pieces

Maple Butter (page 78)

....

NOTE *We use Frontier lemon and orange flavor, which are alcohol-free extracts. If you can't find these flavors, you can substitute lemon and orange zest.*

Our French toast owes its popularity to the brioche we use. High quality and handmade, it is dipped in a special vanilla and citrus batter. After cooking on the griddle, the bread gets light, fluffy, and spongy in the middle and yet crispy on the edges from the butter. It's so airy and soft that we think of it as the workingman's soufflé. Our topping of caramelized bananas, roasted pecans, and warm Maple Butter really takes the old standby — bread and butter — to another level.

1   Preheat the oven to warm, 250°F.

2   Whisk together all of the batter ingredients (eggs through extracts) in a shallow bowl. Dip in each slice of brioche or challah for 5 to 6 seconds per side. Swirl the bread in the batter, but don't soak the bread too long, as both breads are very absorbent. Make sure that the outsides are wet but that the bread is not soaked all the way through.

3   Use either a griddle or flat sauté pan to make the French toast. If using a griddle, melt 1 tablespoon butter on the surface; or if using a sauté pan, melt 4 tablespoons butter until foamy. Add the bread and brown each side until dark golden, about 3 minutes per side (if using a pan, sauté 2 slices at once). Repeat with the remaining slices. Place all the toast on a lightly buttered cookie sheet and place the sheet into a warm oven.

4   Lightly brown 1 tablespoon butter in a separate 9-inch sauté pan over high heat. Once the butter is past the foaming stage, add the brown sugar and cook until melted. Use a spoon to break up any sugar lumps. Add the bananas and mix in until coated. Sprinkle 2 tablespoons of the cinnamon sugar over the bananas. Cook until the bananas become caramelized and golden brown, but not mushy and overcooked. Be careful to keep the pan steady so that the bananas will caramelize.

5   Garnish the warm French toast with caramelized bananas, toasted pecans, and a sprinkling of cinnamon sugar. Serve Maple Butter on the side.

VANILLA *Buttermilk Waffles*

MAKES 8 TO 10 BELGIAN WAFFLES OR 14 REGULAR WAFFLES

Pancake batter (use the batter recipe for Neil's Pancakes, page 75)

1 TABLESPOON *clarified butter (see page 143)*

1 TABLESPOON *canola oil, plus more for the waffle iron*

1 TEASPOON *vanilla extract*

1 TEASPOON *orange extract*

Confectioners' sugar

Pancake Toppings (choose from those on pages 80–84)

Maple Butter (page 78) or Hot Fudge Sauce (page 179)

The key to a perfect waffle is a very hot iron. These waffles are a derivative of our pancake batter — with the addition of some extra clarified butter whipped in and a little bit of oil in the batter so that when it hits the waffle iron, it gets very crispy. And delicious toppings. We adjust ours seasonally: In late summer we do stone fruits like plums, peaches, and nectarines, sautéed with whole roasted almonds. In the middle of summer, we do a simple but beautiful topping of fresh berries with powdered sugar and a touch of Maple Butter (page 78) and crushed pistachios. In the dead of winter, we'll use roasted apples and pears with Cinnamon Sour Cream (page 157). And then in early spring we might do sour cherries. If you want to make a savory waffle, serve it with Honey Tabasco Sauce (page 156) and our Buttermilk Fried Chicken (page 124).

1   Make the pancake batter. Lightly fold in the clarified butter, oil, vanilla, and orange extract. Preheat your waffle iron to 350°F, according to manufacturer's instructions.

2   Once the waffle iron is ready, spray it with nonstick oil or lightly brush it with oil. Cook for 3½ minutes, or until the waffle is golden brown with a nice crust and crunchy texture. Serve right out of the iron onto plates for ultimate crispness, sprinkled with confectioners' sugar and garnished with any of our Pancake Toppings and Maple Butter on the side. For dessert, the waffles go well with a scoop of vanilla ice cream and Hot Fudge Sauce.

5

. SOUPS .

When we first opened the bakery, Neil's focus was
wholesale accounts at small grocers and boutique cafés,
so he made his pastries and biscuits to go.

At the time, Wylie Dufresne, the famed chef, was opening his WD-50 down the street and his father, Dewey (also his wine director) came in often for his morning coffee. He said he and his workers couldn't get lunch anywhere in the neighborhood: "You should make soups." Of course he was right, and Neil went crazy with soups. Word spread fast and before we knew it, calls were coming in every morning asking for the soup of the day. We were shocked at just how many people on the Lower East Side wanted a freshly made soup.

These days our soups at the bakery stand out because of their seasonal ingredients, down-home flavor, and the quality products we use. The Tomato Zucchini Bisque, for example, is an homage to end-of-season tomatoes — and to having too much zucchini on hand. The Lobster Bisque captures the essence of lobster without going overboard on the cream or thickening agents. It's a rustic version of a fancy soup that really exemplifies the flavors a lobster shell will give.

The thing to remember about soups is that they develop over time. They're also inexpensive to make, forgiving of mistakes, and the perfect answer to the dilemma of leftovers. Throw in your stray crudités from a party on Saturday night, liberate your canned beans, chop up your wilting fresh herbs . . . Presto! You've got a meal.

If, like us, you prefer creamy pureed soup, even without the cream, and you don't want to go through the hassle of blending, invest in a beurre mixer or immersion blender, which is a utensil you can put directly into the pot to create the consistency that you desire.

CORN & CLAM *Chowder*

SERVES 8 TO 10

2 CUPS *fresh shucked corn (from about 4 ears)*

1 CUP *heavy cream*

2 TABLESPOONS *extra virgin olive oil*

½ CUP *chopped raw sliced bacon*

3 CLOVES *garlic, smashed and minced*

1 *whole medium sweet onion, minced*

½ TEASPOON *cayenne pepper*

2 *bay leaves*

2 TABLESPOONS *fresh thyme leaves, chopped*

3 TABLESPOONS *all-purpose flour*

3 TABLESPOONS *unsalted butter*

3 *small Idaho potatoes, peeled and cut into big chunks*

2 TABLESPOONS *salt and ground white pepper, blended*

4 CUPS *clam juice*

2 CUPS *chopped clams (frozen or fresh)*

A nod to summer, our Corn & Clam Chowder smacks of a seaside vacation, especially because the kitchen makes a corn stock right from the cobs. This gives it an amazingly rich maize flavor, putting a little spin on the classic clam chowder.

1 First, puree the corn: Put 1 cup of the raw corn and ½ cup of the heavy cream in the bowl of a food processor or blender and pulse or blend until pureed. Set aside.

2 In a medium to large stockpot with a lid, add the olive oil and bacon. Cook on medium to high heat until the bacon is lightly browned and the fat is drawn out. Add the garlic, onion, cayenne pepper, bay leaves, and thyme, and cook for 8 to 10 minutes, until the onion is translucent and soft.

3 Sprinkle the flour over the bacon-and-onion mixture. Stir in the butter and mix until the flour and onions are fully incorporated and make a smooth paste (this roux will slightly thicken the base of the soup). Add the potatoes and the remaining cup of corn and cook for another 5 to 7 minutes. Add the salt and pepper and clam juice, plus 2 cups water. Add the chopped clams and bring the soup to a boil.

4 When the soup is slightly thickened, add the pureed corn mixture and the remaining heavy cream. Do not bring the soup back to a boil. Continue simmering until the potatoes are just cooked. Adjust the seasonings to taste. Remove the bay leaves.

LOBSTER *Bisque*

SERVES 10 TO 14

4 *live lobsters,* 1¼ **POUNDS** *each*

¼ **CUP** *extra virgin olive oil*

1 *medium Spanish onion, halved and then sliced into rounds*

2 *medium carrots, halved lengthwise and sliced thin on the bias*

4 **STALKS** *celery, sliced thin on the bias*

2 *medium leeks (white and light green parts), halved lengthwise and sliced into rounds*

4 *medium-large shallots, sliced into rounds*

4 *bay leaves*

4 **TO** 5 **SPRIGS** *fresh thyme*

4 **TO** 5 **SPRIGS** *fresh tarragon (if not available, use 1 tablespoon dried tarragon)*

6 **CLOVES** *garlic, peeled and smashed*

1 **TEASPOON** *black or white peppercorns*

1 **TEASPOON** *cayenne pepper*

1 **TEASPOON** *saffron*

½ **CUP** *tomato paste*

2 **CUPS** *dry white wine*

½ **CUP** *brandy*

2 **TABLESPOONS** *salt*

½ **TABLESPOON** *ground white pepper*

4 **TABLESPOONS** *unsalted butter, room temperature*

5 **TABLESPOONS** *cornstarch*

1 **CUP** *heavy cream*

Crème fraîche (optional)

This is a no-waste recipe. The shells and lobster bodies give the bisque an authentic, rich lobster flavor, and the tomalleys and roe paste provide an "ocean-y" taste.

1   Plunge an 8- or 10-inch chef's knife or cleaver through the top of where the lobster's head separates from the body, toward the middle of the eyes. This is the quickest, most humane method. The lobster will die instantly, although it may still continue to twitch. (An alternative method is to dunk the lobster in boiling water until it dies, but this is less humane and the bisque is best made with raw shells.) Over a bowl or the sink, twist off the claws and the tail. Cut the remaining body in half and remove the sac (very similar to a shrimp vein) at the very tip of the head (it contains waste and can make your bisque gritty). Repeat the process with the remaining 3 lobsters. With a spoon or your fingers, remove the roe (eggs) and tomalley (green stringy part). Place them in a bowl and reserve. (They will be used as a thickening paste for the bisque toward the end of the cooking process.) Chop the lobster halves horizontally in thirds. If the tentacles or legs are too long, cut them in half.

2   In a large pot, bring 6 to 8 quarts water to boil. Once the water is boiling, boil the tails and claws together for 8 minutes. Use tongs to move the lobster around in the water so that it cooks evenly. Once the lobster is cooked, drain the pieces and plunge them into ice water to stop the cooking process and cool.

3   Begin shelling the tails over a bowl by squeezing them at the top and breaking the back. It can be helpful to use a towel. Crack the heavy part of the claw with the heel of a knife and crack around the whole circumference of the claw. Remove the claw meat in one piece. Slice into the knuckle to halve vertically. Remove the knuckle meat from each side. The tail, claw, or knuckle meat can be sliced and used as a garnish or in a salad, for a lobster roll, or in a Benedict recipe. Reserve both the juice from the lobster as well as shells and bodies.

4   In a separate 10- to 12-quart soup pot with a heavy bottom, warm the olive oil over high heat. Add the reserved lobster heads and shell pieces and sear for 10 minutes, until the heads and shells begin to turn red. Add the vegetables, herbs, and seasonings (onion through saffron). Stir until combined and continue to cook for 10 minutes. Add the tomato paste, wine, ¼ cup of the brandy, and reserved lobster juice to the mixture. Cook for 5 to 7 minutes, until the vegetables are soft and the liquid is reduced by a third.

5   Add 4 quarts water and salt and pepper to the bisque and bring to a boil. Simmer the bisque for 20 minutes. Add the remaining brandy to the roe and tomalleys in order to make the paste. Use a fork to whisk in the butter and 3 tablespoons of the cornstarch. Bring the bisque back to a boil and whisk in the roe paste. Boil the bisque for 5 minutes in order to cook out the taste of cornstarch. Remove the pot from the heat and rest the soup at the back of the stove for 5 minutes to allow the flavors to continue to develop.

6   Place a colander over a large bowl and drain the soup into the bowl. Remove the bay leaves from the colander and blend the remaining solid ingredients using an immersion blender. If you do not have an immersion blender, keep the solid ingredients in the colander and mash vigorously for 5 to 10 minutes, until fine, with a heavy mallet or the back of a small pot. Mix together the smashed ingredients so that they are released through the colander into the liquid, pressing against the holes. Let the colander sit on top of the bowl for a couple of minutes so the liquid continues to seep through to the bisque below.

7   Return the bisque to the same cooking pot and place on the stove and turn the heat to medium-high. Reduce the bisque by a third, for about 20 minutes, over a rolling simmer.

8   Whisk the remaining 2 tablespoons cornstarch into the heavy cream. Whisk this blend into the bisque and cook at a simmer for 5 more minutes. Adjust the seasoning and, using a ladle, strain the soup through a medium or fine strainer. Top with a garnish of lobster pieces and crème fraîche.

SPLIT PEA *Soup*

SERVES 10 TO 12

¼ **CUP** *extra virgin olive oil*

1 **CUP** *finely diced celery*

2 **CUPS** *finely diced carrots*

2 **CUPS** *finely diced onions*

2 **CLOVES** *garlic, smashed*

2 **TABLESPOONS** *chopped fresh thyme leaves*

2 *bay leaves*

1 **CUP** *smoked country ham, diced (alternately, a ham bone)*

1 **POUND** *split peas, rinsed and drained*

3¼ **TABLESPOONS** *salt*

¾ **TABLESPOON** *ground black pepper*

....

NOTE *Five quarts may sound like a lot of water, but the water will allow the peas to puree within the broth, and the soup will take on a completely different texture as it continues to simmer. This amount of water will also ensure that the vegetables remain chunky.*

We like to add salt toward the end because if added too early in the cooking process, the salt can inhibit the split peas from becoming tender.

Over time, this soup will thicken in the refrigerator. To thin it out, mix in a little more water.

There's nothing really outrageous or different about the ingredients in this soup. What makes it special is how long we cook it, allowing plenty of time for the ham to impart its smokiness. Our split pea soup does indeed take a long time to cook down and thicken, but you'll reap the reward: a dead-of-winter, stick-to-the-ribs, lick-the-bottom-of-the-bowl soup that gets better and better day after day.

1   In a large stockpot over medium-high heat, warm the olive oil. Sauté the celery, carrots, onions, garlic, thyme, and bay leaves until tender, or for 5 minutes. Add the ham to the mixture and continue sautéing for 10 more minutes.

2   Stir in the peas, making sure they are incorporated into the mixture. Lower the heat to medium and add 5 quarts (20 cups) water.

3   Bring the soup to a boil and simmer, uncovered, for 1 hour and 30 minutes. Remove the bay leaves. Season with salt and pepper and serve warm.

SPRING PEA PUREE *Soup*

SERVES 8

2 TABLESPOONS *unsalted butter*

1 *medium white onion, sliced thin*

3 CLOVES *garlic, smashed and coarsely chopped*

2½ CUPS *leeks (1 or 2, white and light green parts) halved lengthwise and cut crosswise in ½-inch pieces (see Restaurant Trick, page 93)*

1 *medium-large Yukon gold or Idaho potato, peeled and cut into cubes*

5 CUPS *chicken stock, vegetable stock, or water*

3 CUPS *fresh or frozen peas (fresh peas are in season between May and July)*

2 TEASPOONS *salt*

½ TEASPOON *ground white pepper*

1 CUP *heavy cream*

½ CUP *sour cream or crème fraîche*

½ CUP *minced fresh chives*

The bright, light green color of this soup is very pretty and quite appetizing. All it needs for garnish is a dollop of sour cream or crème fraîche and a sprinkle of minced chives. In summer, serve it chilled. It's our three-year-old daughter's favorite soup.

1   Melt the butter over medium-high heat in a 6- to 8-quart heavy-bottomed stockpot.

2   Cook the onion, garlic, and leeks for 3 to 4 minutes, until glistening and soft (lower the heat if they start to brown).

3   Add the potato and stir for 1 minute, until coated with the vegetables.

4   Add the stock or water and cook on high heat until boiling. Turn down the heat to medium and simmer for 15 to 20 minutes, until the potato is cooked through. Add the peas and cook for another 5 minutes.

5   Add salt and pepper. Add the cream, cook for 1 minute, and turn off the heat.

6   Using a ladle, transfer the soup to a blender and blend at medium, then high speed, for 1 to 2 minutes. Be very careful with the hot liquid. Keep the cover on tight. (Neil likes to place a towel over the blender lid. You might have to blend this soup in two batches if your blender holds only 1 quart.)

7   After all soup is blended, pour it back into the pot and adjust the seasoning with salt and pepper to taste. Serve in bowls with a dollop of sour cream or crème fraîche and a sprinkle of chives.

MAPLE BUTTER ROASTED *Squash Soup*

SERVES 10 TO 12

2 *medium to large butternut squash*

1 CUP *Maple Butter (page 78), plus more for drizzling*

2 *cinnamon sticks*

4 *whole cloves*

1 POD *star anise*

2 *bay leaves*

4 SPRIGS *fresh thyme (including stems)*

ONE 20-BY-20-INCH *cheesecloth square*

2 TABLESPOONS *unsalted butter*

1 TABLESPOON *canola or vegetable oil*

1 CUP *chopped onions*

1 CUP *chopped carrots*

½ CUP *chopped celery*

2 *medium leeks (white and light green parts), sliced (see Restaurant Trick, page 93)*

2 CLOVES *garlic, smashed*

1 CUP *white wine*

¼ CUP *Maker's Mark or Jack Daniel's bourbon*

6 CUPS *or more vegetable stock or water*

2 TABLESPOONS *salt*

½ TABLESPOON *ground black pepper*

This is a rich and special soup, worthy of a great dinner party or momentous meal. The Maple Butter adds unique flavor to the soup and makes it quite addictive.

Most squash soup recipes instruct you to peel, seed, and chop the squash, a really arduous task, especially when the squash is very hard. But with this soup, all you need to do is split the squash in half, remove the seeds, and throw it in the oven with a little Maple Butter.

The rest is simple: After you cook the squash, cool it, scoop the flesh out of the shell, and it's done. The roasting is the key with this soup, as it imparts a nice autumnal note.

Although there is at least an hour of prep time for the standard home cook, you can make this soup a day or two in advance, and then you're good to go, whether you're expecting company or need a quick weeknight meal. The flavors will only grow more complex over time.

1   Preheat the oven to 375°F.

2   Split each squash lengthwise and scoop out the seeds with a spoon. Separate out the seeds from any stringy pulp and reserve them for a garnish (see cooking instructions on page 99). Halve each squash piece horizontally so that you have a total of 8 pieces of squash. Use a large spoon to hollow out the top piece of each squash (the pieces that have no seed cavity) just enough to fill with Maple Butter. Place the extra flesh, hollowed out with the spoon, in the bottom cavity of each squash so that no squash is wasted. Arrange the squash pieces on a large sheet pan, cut side up, and pour 1 tablespoon of Maple Butter into each squash cavity (8 tablespoons of Maple Butter total). Bake for 45 minutes or until tender. To test if the squash is tender, insert a knife into the flesh. If it sinks in easily and the squash is golden brown, it's ready to be removed from the oven.

(continued on page 99)

In Neil's first cooking class at New York Tech, the first thing he learned was *mise en place*: everything in its place. Shallots minced, veal stock reduced, cheese grated, tomatoes diced. This preparation for the "service" was the most important aspect of cooking in a real kitchen. If you didn't have all the items ready when an order came through the printer, you were screwed.

Whether you're serving a banquet hall or a breakfast for two, the same philosophy should apply. Have your meat or fish portioned properly, your butter clarified, your thyme leaves picked, your olive oil uncapped. Without your ingredients within reach and within sight, it is virtually impossible to organize yourself and serve a decent meal.

The first way to get your *mise* prepared is to read the recipe and do a mental or physical checklist of everything needed. With your *mise* in place, the kitchen will run like a well-oiled machine, and no matter how busy you get you'll never get stuck, as chefs like to say, "in the weeds."

NOTE *To save time, you can chop your vegetables for step 5 while the squash is roasting.*

3 Once the squash is roasted, allow it to cool and scoop the flesh from the skins with a spoon. Discard the skins.

4 Prepare the bouquet garni sachet. Place the spices and herbs in the middle of the cheesecloth. Bring all of the corners to the center and twist them together. Tie the twist into a knot or secure the cheesecloth with a piece of kitchen twine.

5 In a large stockpot, warm the butter and oil over medium-high heat, and cook the vegetables for approximately 5 to 8 minutes. Add the garlic and the bouquet garni and sauté the mixture until the vegetables are translucent, approximately 5 to 8 minutes.

6 Add the white wine and reduce the liquid by half. Remove the pot from the stove and add the bourbon. Light a match over the pot to flambé the mixture, being very careful! The soup will flame. Allow the alcohol to cook off.

7 Add the roasted squash and 6 cups vegetable stock or water to the mixture and stir to combine. Bring the soup to a boil and simmer for 15 minutes. Add the salt and pepper and adjust the seasoning to taste.

8 Remove the bouquet garni from the soup with tongs. Use a blender to puree the soup in 4 parts. (Be very careful with the hot liquid. Keep the cover on tight. Neil likes to place a towel over the blender lid.) If the mixture is too thick, add more stock or water to thin it out. While the soup is blending, add 2 tablespoons Maple Butter through the top of the blender (8 tablespoons in total) to the soup. You may need to help the blender by turning it off and stirring the soup every 15 to 30 seconds. Serve the soup warm and top with a drizzle of Maple Butter and a sprinkling of Butternut Squash Seeds.

Butternut Squash Seeds

1 Preheat the oven to 375°F.

2 Scatter the seeds evenly on a cookie sheet. Generously salt the seeds and roast for 8 to 10 minutes, until toasted.

3 Use as soup garnish or eat as a snack.

TURKEY *Chili*

SERVES 8 TO 10

1 1/2 **TABLESPOONS** *extra virgin olive oil*

1 *medium Spanish onion, diced*

2 *medium carrots, diced*

3 **STALKS** *celery, diced*

1 *medium red bell pepper, diced*

3 **CLOVES** *garlic, minced*

1 **POUND** *ground turkey*

1 1/2 **TABLESPOONS** *chili powder*

1/2 **TABLESPOON** *garlic powder*

1/2 **TABLESPOON** *dried oregano*

1/2 **TABLESPOON** *cumin*

1/2 **TEASPOON** *dried thyme*

1/2 **TEASPOON** *red pepper flakes*

2 *bay leaves*

2 **SHAKES** *Tabasco sauce*

1 **TABLESPOON** *tomato paste*

1/2 **TABLESPOON** *chipotle peppers in adobo sauce*

3 **CUPS** *crushed tomatoes*

2 **CUPS** *chicken stock*

2 **CUPS (15-OUNCE CAN)** *cooked kidney beans in liquid*

1 1/4 **TABLESPOONS** *salt*

1/4 **TABLESPOON** *ground black pepper*

Optional garnishes: shredded cheddar cheese, Jalapeño Sour Cream (page 156), Guacamole (page 154), and fried tortilla strips (or crushed tortilla chips)

....

NOTE *The ground turkey doesn't have to be perfectly broken up. Big chunks are fine. In fact, these chunks will add great flavor to the soup.*

Spicy, complex, totally addictive, this chili is one of our biggest sellers, especially on a cold winter's day. We serve it with shredded cheddar, Jalapeño Sour Cream (page 156), and a few crispy tortilla strips. Throw in a spoonful of Guacamole (page 154) and you've got a hearty, satisfying meal. Bonus: this stew will taste even better the next day. For a big crowd, just double this recipe!

1   In a large stockpot over medium-high heat, warm the olive oil and cook the vegetables and garlic in the oil until tender. Don't be afraid to caramelize the vegetables a little bit. Add the turkey to the mixture, breaking up the ground meat with a spoon until the turkey is cooked and colors slightly.

2   Add the herbs and spices, Tabasco, and tomato paste to the mixture and stir until combined. Stir the peppers in adobo sauce into the crushed tomatoes and add both to the pot. Pour in the chicken stock, bring to a boil, and simmer for 15 minutes.

3   Add the kidney beans and their liquid to the stew and cook for 5 minutes or until the beans are warmed through. (If you want a less soupy chili, just cook it down until it's reached your desired consistency.) Season with salt and pepper. Remove bay leaves and serve warm with your choice of garnishes.

TOMATO *Zucchini Bisque*

SERVES 8 TO 10

¼ CUP *extra virgin olive oil*

1 CUP *diced carrots (2 medium)*

4 CUPS *diced zucchini (3–4 medium)*

1 CUP *diced red onion
(half a medium onion)*

1 CUP *diced white onion
(half a medium)*

1 CUP *diced celery*

6 CLOVES *garlic, smashed*

3 TABLESPOONS *fresh thyme
leaves, roughly chopped (or rubbed
straight off the stem)*

2 *bay leaves*

PINCH *of red pepper flakes*

4 CUPS (APPROXIMATELY
TWO 28-OUNCE CANS) *crushed
Italian peeled plum tomatoes*

2 TEASPOONS *salt*

½ TEASPOON *ground black pepper*

2 CUPS *heavy cream (optional)*

....

NOTE   *If in season, use fresh
chopped plum or Roma tomatoes in
place of the canned tomatoes.*

*If you cannot find crushed tomatoes
in your grocery store, buy canned
whole tomatoes and use your hands
to crush the tomatoes into the soup.*

NOTE   *You can cut down the
cream — or omit it if you want
a dairy-free soup.*

This beautiful soup has a velvety texture. At the restaurant we serve it with a Grilled Goat Cheese Sandwich (page 115) on the side, making it a perfect meal. Cue some cold weather or an icy rain, and there's nothing better than a day inside with this soup on your stove.

1   In a large stockpot with a covered lid, warm the olive oil over medium-high heat. Cook the vegetables and garlic with the herbs and pepper flakes until tender (about 10 to 12 minutes). Stir the vegetables often, until well coated in the oil, making sure they do not burn.

2   Turn the heat down to medium, remove the lid, and add the tomatoes and 4 cups water. Bring the soup to a boil and then simmer for 20 minutes.

3   Season the soup with the salt and pepper and remove the bay leaves.

4   Remove the pot from the stove. Blend half of the soup in a blender for 2 to 3 minutes or until smooth. (Be very careful with the hot liquid. Keep the cover on tight. Neil likes to place a towel over the blender lid.) Add 1 cup of the heavy cream directly to the soup through the top part of the blender while blending. Blend the second half of the soup using the same method and the remaining cream.

5   Combine all the soup and push it through a fine strainer or China cap (a triangular funnel with a metal frame) set over a large bowl or pot, for a finer consistency. Adjust the seasoning to taste and serve warm.

ANDOUILLE SAUSAGE *Gumbo*

SERVES 10 TO 12

4 TABLESPOONS *unsalted butter*

10 TABLESPOONS *all-purpose flour*

1 *medium Spanish onion, diced*

1 *large red bell pepper, diced*

1 *large green bell pepper, diced*

3 STALKS *celery, diced*

4 *medium to large cloves garlic, chopped*

2 TABLESPOONS *fresh thyme leaves*

2 *bay leaves*

½ TEASPOON *cayenne pepper*

2 TABLESPOONS *salt (preferably kosher)*

1 TEASPOON *ground black pepper*

4 CUPS *andouille sausage slices, ¼-inch thick*

Shrimp Stock (recipe follows)

12 *okra* (**2 CUPS**) *sliced into ½-inch slices (frozen okra is acceptable if fresh is not available)*

1 *large tomato, cut into ¼-inch chunks*

1½ CUPS *scallions (1 bunch), cut into ¼-inch pieces*

1 CUP *cooked white rice*

This soup is all about the roux. That's what gives the gumbo its color, complexity, and nutty flavor. Once you master the art of a roux, the soup is foolproof. This gumbo is a great base for any other protein that you might want to add: try shrimp, crabmeat, chicken, or duck.

1   Melt butter in a small-cast iron or heavy-bottomed sauté pan. Add the flour and stir with a wooden spoon to make a smooth paste. Cook over medium-low heat for 15 to 20 minutes. Stir. Turn up the heat to medium-high and cook for another 10 minutes while stirring. The roux should get foamy and start to smell nutty and turn light brown. Continue stirring until the roux turns chocolate brown, another 10 minutes. It is important to see the stages in a roux from blond, to light brown, to dark brown, to chocolate brown. This will determine the color, flavor, and complexity of the gumbo. If it goes too fast, too soon, it will burn before it reaches the chocolate brown stage.

2   Transfer the hot roux to an 8- to 10-quart stockpot. Add onion, peppers, celery, and garlic and cook over medium heat until the veggies start to soften and cook with the roux, approximately 10 minutes. Add the thyme, bay leaves, cayenne, salt, and pepper. Cook for 5 minutes, add the sausage, and cook for another 5 minutes. Add the Shrimp Stock and stir well. Cook until boiling, then simmer for 20 to 30 minutes, until the gumbo starts to thicken. Add the okra, continue cooking for another 10 minutes, and adjust the seasonings. Add the chopped tomato, scallions, and cooked rice. Stir well and remove the bay leaves before serving.

3 **CUPS** *shrimp shells (from peeled, fresh or frozen shrimp)*

1 **CUP** *white wine*

1 *medium Spanish onion, sliced thin*

2 **STALKS** *celery*

2 *medium carrots*

1 **TABLESPOON** *tomato paste*

2 **CLOVES** *garlic, smashed*

½ **BUNCH** *fresh parsley*

2 **SPRIGS** *fresh thyme*

2 *bay leaves*

2 **TABLESPOONS** *whole black peppercorns*

1 **TEASPOON** *salt*

Shrimp Stock

Bring all ingredients to a boil in a 2-gallon stockpot with 6 cups water. Turn down heat and simmer for 20 minutes. Strain and reserve the liquid for gumbo.

6

THE SANDWICH
KING & QUEEN

Neil got his start in a crazy kitchen in Flatbush, Brooklyn, among three siblings, two parents, sixteen neighborhood cousins, and six aunts and uncles. At ten years old, he became a culinary boy wonder who'd do anything to avoid his mother's "famous" dish, chicken in a pot (the only dish in her repertoire).

His sandwiches, made assembly line style for his relatives, were the stuff of legend on Avenue J. Even Dr. Ginsberg, Neil's pediatrician, was lured to the Kleinberg two-family residence for a taste of his famous egg salad. "Could it be any creamier?" asked Neil's mother, Millie (rhetorically, of course). Neil kept his masterpieces simple and classic: tuna salad on rye toast with crisp lettuce and beefsteak tomatoes, fresh corned beef with mustard and sauerkraut, turkey and Swiss with Russian dressing and coleslaw.

As a kid, my favorite sandwich was salami on rye with mayonnaise. At home I got away with it, but at Rein's delicatessen, where I once asked for it loud and proud, my mother raised her brows, and said, "People don't order that." (Not Jewish people, anyway.) By the time I hit the college cafeteria, I'd turned a corner — my friends crowned me the Sandwich Queen. I could craft something out of blue cheese, alfalfa sprouts, and cucumbers and make it look good. It was partly what I put on the sandwich (Havarti with honey mustard, egg salad with bacon bits), but even more how I piled and layered it to maximize texture, color, and crunch.

Today our favorite sandwiches in New York include the lobster roll at Pearl Oyster Bar (the buttery toasted bread, the fresh chunks of lobster meat tossed with just a little mayo to hold it together, a *pluche* of greens . . . it's summer vacation on a bun); Katz's hand-carved pastrami on rye with lots of deli mustard; Defonte's potato and egg sandwich with Virginia ham, salt, pepper, and ketchup (Neil's top pick), and their own mozzarella with roast beef and fried eggplant (mine); Faicco's Italian hero — a whopping torpedo of sliced porkiness; the delicious meatballs studded with pignolis on rosemary flatbread at Frankie's on Clinton; the delectable shrimp salad on dense Irish raisin soda bread at Serendipity (my childhood beloved); and, of course, our favorite Clinton St. staple: the classic Po' Boy (page 108). A medium-thick whitefish fillet, crunchy and crisp on the outside, moist and tender in the middle; a bit of cornmeal flavor from the breading; slathered with our own Tartar Sauce; chock full of capers, Lower East Side pickles, fresh herbs, and Hellmann's mayo. It's the Rolls-Royce of fish fillet sandwiches.

WHITE TUNA FISH *Sandwiches*

MAKES 4 SANDWICHES

THREE 5-OUNCE CANS *solid white tuna, packed in water*

1 STALK *celery*

⅓ CUP *finely diced white onion (quarter of a medium onion)*

¾ CUP *mayonnaise, such as Hellmann's or Best Foods*

PINCH *of salt*

PINCH *of white ground pepper*

1 TEASPOON *freshly squeezed lemon juice*

8 SLICES *rye bread*

8 (¼-INCH-THICK) SLICES *tomato*

12 TO 16 *romaine lettuce leaves or mixed greens*

In any Jewish household in Brooklyn in the 1960s, tuna salad was the number one sandwich. You had to learn how to make a good one to survive. Neil always thought his was the best. What set his apart was the fact that he liked to cut the celery and onion really fine and mix the tuna with his hands until it was the texture of fine wood shavings. Along with the mayo and a touch of salt and pepper, a splash of lemon juice balances the flavors.

1   Drain the cans of tuna so that most of the water is removed. Place the tuna in a large mixing bowl. With a vegetable peeler or knife, peel the top layer off the celery stalk (this layer can be stringy). Finely dice. Add the celery and onion dice to the tuna. Add the mayonnaise, salt, pepper, and lemon juice. Mix together the ingredients with gloved or clean hands. Crush together the mixture with your fingers until well combined, making sure to break up large chunks of tuna.

2   Toast the bread.

3   Assemble each sandwich with ⅔ cup tuna salad, 3 to 4 pieces of lettuce, and 2 slices of tomato.

4   Serve with potato chips and a pickle.

PO' BOYS

MAKES 2 SANDWICHES

TWO *4- to 6-ounce fillets seasonal flatfish (see Note)*

Salt

Pepper

....

STATION 1

½ **CUP** *all-purpose flour*

½ **TEASPOON** *salt*

PINCH *of ground white pepper*

¼ **TEASPOON** *cayenne pepper*

....

STATION 2

1 *large egg*

1 TABLESPOON *water*

PINCH *of salt*

....

STATION 3

½ **CUP** *panko breadcrumbs*

½ **CUP** *ground cornmeal*

PINCH *of salt*

3 TO 4 TABLESPOONS *canola oil*

2 ciabatta *or white French rolls, roughly the same size as the fish fillets*

4 TEASPOONS *unsalted butter*

2 TO 4 LEAVES *romaine or other green-leaf lettuce*

4 TABLESPOONS *Tartar Sauce (page 164), plus more for serving*

The Po' Boy is not only our favorite sandwich at the restaurant, but the favorite of many of our staff, both front and back of house. Part of the appeal is the amazing bread we use, which is an old-school French roll that — when toasted on the griddle with butter — gets quite crispy on the outside while retaining its soft and moist inside. We change up our fish day to day, but some of the most popular are flounder, catfish, and soft-shell crabs.

1   Preheat the oven to 350°F.

2   Season the fish fillets on both sides with salt and pepper. Have a cookie sheet lined with parchment paper or foil ready. Set up your three stations in order in shallow baking dishes or bowls. Use a whisk to combine each set of ingredients. If the cornmeal in Station 3 settles to the bottom, mix it with a whisk before you use it. If the panko has large pieces, break them up with your fingers.

NOTE *We like to use haddock, pollock, catfish, or tilapia. These fillets tend to be ½- to ¾-inch thick, in which case you should finish cooking them for 5 to 7 minutes, until cooked through, in a 350°F oven. We also use flounder or fluke, which is often sold as thinner fillets. If you use either of these fish, it needs to finish cooking in the 350°F oven for only 3 to 4 minutes.*

RESTAURANT TRICK *The flour mixture seals in the moisture of the fillet and creates a space between the fillet and the panko and cornmeal coating. This process will create a nice, crispy coating without becoming greasy. To make the coating process easier, glove one hand so that you always have a free and clean hand.*

You can tell if the oil has reached the perfect temperature by placing a small cube of bread in the pan. If it sizzles in the oil and browns quickly, the oil is ready for the fillets.

3   Dredge the fish in the flour mixture (Station 1), shake off the excess flour, and then dip the fillets into the egg mixture (Station 2) until coated. Let any excess moisture drip off. Roll the fillets in the panko and cornmeal mixture (Station 3) until well coated. Place both fillets on the cookie sheet.

4   In a 10-inch oven-safe skillet, heat the oil over medium-low heat until the oil is shimmering and coats the pan in a thin layer. Sauté the fillets for 2 to 3 minutes on each side until the crust becomes golden brown. Finish the fillets in the oven. See the Note for cooking times.

5   While the fillets bake, slice the rolls in half and butter each half with 1 teaspoon butter. Toast the bread in the oven until crisp and the butter is melted.

6   Remove the fish from the oven and drain and pat dry with a paper towel. Smear each roll half with 1 teaspoon Tartar Sauce and then place the fish on top of the bottom half of each roll. Use your hand to flatten out the ribs in the lettuce and place 1 to 2 pieces on top of the fish. Place the top half of the roll on top of the lettuce. Slice each sandwich in half on the diagonal. Serve with potato chips, Coleslaw (page 134), a pickle, and extra Tartar Sauce on the side.

VEGGIE *Sandwich*

MAKES 1 SANDWICH

2 SLICES *seven grain or whole grain bread*

HALF *an avocado, pitted*

2 TABLESPOONS *Herb Mayo (page 157)*

PINCH *of salt*

PINCH *of freshly ground white pepper*

3 TO 4 LEAVES *mixed green lettuce*

3 (¼-INCH-THICK) SLICES *tomato*

½ CUP *alfalfa sprouts, loosely packed*

2 SLICES *Muenster cheese*

This sandwich was inspired by the first real veggie sandwich I ever had, at a popular health food restaurant in east midtown Manhattan called Au Natural. My grandmother lived nearby, and Au Natural was our staple, pre- or post-Bloomingdale's. It was the first place I ever tried an avocado. Back then, in the fourth grade, I didn't realize they were part of a new movement called California cuisine.

Neil loves to tell me about his first experience with avocado, in Lake Tahoe. He was seventeen and everyone ate theirs mashed with a little salt and pepper, garlic powder, and a touch of mayo, then spread out on "freaky" whole grain bread. For both of us, the avocado was a revelation. It's hard to believe now that this succulent fruit is commonplace.

Some of our guests love this sandwich with bacon, perhaps defeating the whole purpose, but it is an amazing addition so we cannot begrudge them. Naturally, a side of Neil's Coleslaw (page 134) is the perfect accompaniment on the plate.

1   Toast the bread. Scoop the avocado flesh out of the shell with a large spoon or peel the avocado and place the flat side down on a cutting board. Slice the flesh into long thin slices and push it to one side to fan the slices. Match the size of the fanned avocado to the size of your bread. Reserve the remaining avocado for another use (see Guacamole, page 154) and squeeze lemon juice over it to prevent it from browning.

2   Spread each slice of toast with 1 tablespoon Herb Mayo. Arrange the avocado slices on top of the mayonnaise on one slice of toast. Sprinkle the avocado with salt and pepper. Use your fingers to press down lightly on the avocado so it adheres to the toast and mayonnaise. Place the lettuce on top of the avocado and then the tomato slices, sprouts, and cheese. Top the sandwich with the second slice of toast, mayonnaise side down. Press on the sandwich to make it compact.

3   Slice the sandwich in half on the diagonal and serve it with mixed greens, Coleslaw (page 134), and a pickle.

CLINTON ST. BURGERS

SERVES 4

FOUR 8-OUNCE HAMBURGER PATTIES *(75% lean sirloin, 25% fatty chuck)*

Kosher salt, for seasoning

Freshly ground black pepper, for seasoning

½ CUP *Caramelized Onions (recipe follows)*

4 *brioche rolls, split, buttered (1 teaspoon unsalted butter on each side) and toasted (facedown on the grill is best)*

8 MEDIUM-THIN SLICES *Swiss cheese*

We're always searching for the best burger. The famed Corner Bistro, located on my very own bachelorette block in Manhattan, was a favorite when I was in my twenties. I later discovered the Shake Shack burger with extra onions and pickles. Neil's favorite is at Peter Luger, made from the scraps of that prime dry-aged short loin and available only at lunch. He also likes Nice Matin's Comté-dripping five-napkin burger, ordered special with a dollop of béarnaise.

Our succulent grass-fed burger at Community Food & Juice, our second restaurant, has a loyal fan base. And *Time Out New York* voted our Clinton St. Burger one of the best in the city, probably because of the 75/25 rule: 75 percent great-quality sirloin combined with 25 percent fatty chuck. Then there's the way we dress it up.

Here's the system with our condiments: First we put the caramelized onions on the burger; second, cheese goes on top of the onions. When the cheese melts on the outside, it makes a seal between the burger and the onions, so you get that perfect bite — char-cooked meat, sweet onions, sharpness of cheese. And then there's the perfectly toasted bun, done the way we like it: buttered and griddled so that the inside of the roll is soft, but the outside crust is a little crunchy, which means a juicy burger won't leave you with a soggy bun.

Last but not least is a genuine Lower East Side pickle from the Pickle Guys. It's perfectly sour and complements the sweetness, the sharpness, and the beautiful flavor of the meat. To round it all out, a forkful of our creamy Coleslaw (page 134) with the crunch of a few potato chips. What could be better than that?

1 Prepare a medium-hot fire in a charcoal grill or preheat a gas grill to medium-high.

2 Season both sides of the burgers with salt and pepper and place on the hottest part of the grill.

3 Grill each side for 6 minutes for medium-rare to medium burgers.

4 Place the 2 tablespoons Caramelized Onions on the cooked burger, then 2 slices Swiss cheese. Place in a toaster oven or in the broiler to melt the cheese.

5 Let the burgers rest for 1 minute before putting them on the buns. Serve with Coleslaw, potato chips, and a Lower East Side pickle.

2 TABLESPOONS *canola oil*

1 TABLESPOON *unsalted butter*

4 *medium to large Vidalia or Spanish onions, thinly sliced*

Salt and ground black pepper

COMMON MISTAKES *The most common mistakes in burger making are pressing down on the burger, which squeezes out all the juice, and cooking it at the wrong temperature.*

NOTE *Try to find Martin's Potato Rolls. If your supermarket or grocer doesn't carry them, get any traditional burger rolls that you like, or even English muffins (sandwich size works best).*

We prefer a real, full-sour Lower East Pickle over any other cuke, but you can use whatever style you like — classic jarred dill or ridged bread-and-butter chips or those spicy vinegar pickles most beloved down South.

Caramelized Onions

MAKES 2 CUPS

The slow cooking of these onions is what makes them melt in your mouth.

1   Over medium-high heat, heat the oil and butter in a large skillet until the butter begins to foam. Add the onions all at once. Turn the heat down to medium-low.

2   Toss the onions every 2 to 3 minutes with tongs or a spoon and continue to cook on medium-low heat. Salt and pepper to taste.

3   The onions will take about 20 minutes to caramelize.

GRILLED GOAT CHEESE *Sandwiches*

MAKES 4 SANDWICHES

8 SLICES *sourdough bread*

8 TABLESPOONS *goat cheese, preferably a creamy cheese from Vermont*

4 TEASPOONS *unsalted butter*

A tiny twist on a simple classic makes this grilled cheese a bit more special and grown-up. Plus, the sourdough bread is a great complement to the goat cheese. At Clinton St., we serve this sandwich with Tomato Zucchini Bisque (page 101).

1   Spread each of 4 slices bread with 2 tablespoons goat cheese. Top with the remaining slices of bread to make sandwiches.

2   Melt 2 teaspoons butter in a pan or griddle on medium heat until foamy. Place 2 sandwiches in the pan and cook for 2 minutes per side, until golden brown. Repeat the process to cook all of the sandwiches.

3   Remove the crusts (optional) and slice horizontally into thirds to make tea-sized sandwiches.

THE REAL *Turkey Sandwich*

MAKES 4 SANDWICHES

⅓ CUP *ketchup*

⅔ CUP *Tartar Sauce (page 164)*

8 SLICES *rye bread, toasted*

2 POUNDS *fresh turkey breast meat, sliced thin*

2 CUPS *Coleslaw (page 134), plus more for serving*

16 THIN SLICES *Swiss cheese*

This is a hearty, fantastic, and filling sandwich, modeled after the quintessential delicatessen version. If you prefer your sandwich lighter, use about 5 ounces (a third of a pound) of turkey per serving.

1   Mix the ketchup with the Tartar Sauce to make Russian dressing. Spread 2 tablespoons Russian dressing on each slice of bread.

2   Top each of 4 slices of the bread with ½ pound turkey, scant ½ cup Coleslaw, and 4 slices Swiss cheese. Top each with the remaining 4 slices bread to make sandwiches. Serve with potato chips, extra Coleslaw on the side, and pickles.

CRAB CAKE *Sandwiches*

MAKES 4 SANDWICHES

1 *large egg, beaten*

1 **TABLESPOON** *freshly squeezed lemon juice*

¾ **CUP** *fresh white breadcrumbs*

1 **TABLESPOON** *chopped fresh parsley*

1 **TABLESPOON** *chopped capers*

1 **TABLESPOON** *minced Spanish onion*

¼ **CUP** *mayonnaise, such as Hellmann's or Best Foods*

1 **TEASPOON** *Dijon mustard*

PINCH *of cayenne pepper*

1 **TEASPOON** *salt*

¼ **TEASPOON** *ground white pepper*

1 **POUND** *lump crabmeat*

2 **TEASPOONS** *canola oil*

4 *brioche buns*

8 **TEASPOONS** *unsalted butter*

½ **CUP** *or more Cajun Remoulade (page 159)*

8 **LEAVES** *lettuce*

8 **THIN SLICES** *beefsteak tomato*

The best crabmeat is always the most expensive, but it's worth the splurge.

1   Preheat the oven to 350°F.

2   Mix together the egg, lemon juice, ½ cup of the breadcrumbs, parsley, capers, and onion with the mayonnaise, mustard, and seasonings. Fold in the crabmeat and shape four 4- to 5-ounce cakes with your hands. Dredge the cakes in the remaining ¼ cup breadcrumbs.

3   In a sauté pan, heat the canola oil, until shimmering, over medium-high heat. Sauté the crab cakes in the pan, flipping after 2 minutes. The crab cakes will be golden brown and crisp. Allow them to cook 2 more minutes and then place on a sheet pan. Place the pan in the oven and bake for 3 to 4 minutes, until the crab cakes are heated all the way through. Drain the crab cakes on a paper-towel-lined plate.

4   While the crab cakes are baking, split the brioche buns and smear each half with 1 teaspoon butter. Bake the rolls in the oven until toasted. Cover the bottom part of each bun with 1 tablespoon or more Cajun Remoulade, 2 lettuce leaves, and 2 slices of tomato on top. Lightly season the tomato with salt and pepper. Place a crab cake, an additional tablespoon or more Cajun Remoulade, and a bun top on each sandwich.

5   Serve with potato chips, Coleslaw (page 134), and a sour pickle, preferably from the Lower East Side.

6½

. FRIED CHICKEN .

{ A CLINTON ST. SPECIALTY }

The fried chicken dinner at Clinton St. is a signature meal; in fact it's so special that we devoted a small chapter just to this dish. It's pretty hard to screw up fried chicken — most deep-fried foods taste reasonably good — but in our restaurant, Neil didn't want to squeak by with average fried food.

No plebeian, greasy drumsticks for him, thank you very much. He wanted to serve fried chicken that tasted fresh, authentic, and super juicy. More than anything, he wanted the spices to come through in the skin, and he wanted the texture of the coating to be absolutely addictive. The solution: a great-quality chicken, brined in a flavorful marinade and fried up remarkably crunchy. To round it out, we add side dishes that meet the highest standards and make the entire meal memorable.

For us it all starts with the quality of the bird. We get the best breed of chicken. At the restaurant we use "Buddhist-style" (head and feet on) Bo Bo chickens, but Murray's or Bell & Evans free-roaming or organic chickens are a good substitute. They promise a clean flavor and dark meat that is always firm, never stringy, and fully contends with the white.

Next is how we prep the chicken. In the South, most cooks simply season it, dredge it in flour, and fry it up either in lard or peanut oil. We marinate our chicken in buttermilk for up to two days, which ensures that the skin, meat, and bones fully absorb the spices. No matter how much you overcook brined chicken, it will turn out juicy and flavorful. It's foolproof. Our flour mixture is also not what you might find down South. The addition of some cornmeal gives it a nice sandy texture and a little bit of corn flavor. There's also enough salt and pepper in the mix for perfect seasoning. You won't have to add one shake at the table.

Last is the frying technique. Ours is simple: we use canola oil instead of peanut oil because it has a neutral flavor, fries at the highest temperature, and gives the chicken a clean, crisp taste without being greasy. Even if you fry the chicken in a Dutch oven instead of a professional deep fryer, you will be amazed at how crispy, crunchy, and satisfying it turns out. It even holds up the next day, cold, which is how we guarantee you'll eat it — straight out of the fridge.

BUTTERMILK *Fried Chicken*

**MAKES 10 PIECES
(4 TO 5 SERVINGS)**

ONE *3- to 3½-pound free-range chicken (preferably Murray's or Bell & Evans) or 10 pieces: 2 wings, 2 thighs, 2 drumsticks, 4 breasts*

....

BUTTERMILK MARINADE

2 CUPS *buttermilk*

2 TEASPOONS *salt*

1 TEASPOON *cayenne pepper*

1 TEASPOON *onion powder*

1 TEASPOON *ground black or white pepper*

1 TEASPOON *garlic powder*

1 TEASPOON *dried thyme*

....

FLOUR & CORNMEAL COATING

2½ CUPS *all-purpose flour*

½ CUP *yellow cornmeal*

2 TABLESPOONS *salt*

2 TEASPOONS *ground black or white pepper*

....

Canola oil, for frying (about 6 cups)

Honey Tabasco Sauce (page 156)

Jalapeño Cornbread (page 45)

Coleslaw (page 134)

We brine the chicken in buttermilk and season it with a variety of spices, including onion powder and cayenne. Serve it with Honey Tabasco Sauce, creamy Coleslaw, and Jalapeño Cornbread. You'll never buy a bucket again.

1 Butcher the chicken, if whole. Place the chicken breast side up on a cutting board. Pull the legs apart to disjoint them. Use your knife to cut the legs from the body, remembering to include the oyster (at the underside of the chicken right below the thigh joint). Cut the drumsticks from the thighs at the joint. Finish the thighs according to the Restaurant Trick that follows.

2 Cut the wings at the breasts. Keep the tip on the wings.

3 Cut the backbone from the chicken and reserve it for stock, or discard. Place the chicken breasts skin-side down on the cutting board with the breastbone facing you. Use a knife to cut a slit in the middle of the breast-bone. Whack with the heel of the knife on either side to loosen the bone. Turn upside down, then peel the breastbone from the breasts and discard. Cut each breast in half on the bias so that the meatier top portion of the breast is smaller than the bottom portion.

4 Whisk together the marinade ingredients in a large bowl. Add the chicken pieces to the marinade and coat well. Store in an airtight container for 3 to 4 hours in the fridge.

5 Whisk together the coating ingredients in a large bowl.

6 Remove the chicken pieces from the marinade (do not drain off the marinade) and dredge in the coating, piece by piece. Coat well, covering all the nooks and crannies. Set aside on a plate. Reserve any extra coating mix.

7 Fill a large cast-iron Dutch oven or cast-iron sauté pan with canola oil halfway. Heat the oil to 350°F over medium heat, using a candy thermometer to make sure the temperature is accurate. Heating may take 8 to 10 minutes.

NOTE *When dredging in flour, use one hand only to keep the other clean and ready for frying.*

RESTAURANT TRICK *Place the thigh skin-side down on a cutting board. Use the heel of the knife to whack through the middle of the thighbone. This will help the chicken cook faster because it won't have to cook through the bone. Additionally, more marinade will penetrate the chicken and you will lessen the chance of blood spots.*

HINT *When removing the chicken from the oil, keep the tips of your tongs facedown to avoid burning yourself. Hold the chicken over the pot briefly to drain off excess oil.*

8 With tongs, gently place the chicken skin-side down in the oil and fry the chicken in batches of 5 to 6 pieces so that they do not crowd the pan. Fry each piece 7 to 8 minutes per side (14 to 16 minutes total cooking time). The wings might take fewer minutes per side. Once cooked on both sides, the chicken will be a dark golden brown and crispy. Be careful when removing the chicken from the oil. It will be very hot. Drain the chicken on a paper-towel-lined sheet pan or place on top of a paper bag. After your first batch, the temperature of the oil will dip. Before adding the second batch, bring the oil back to 350°F. If the batter absorbs all the coating and the chicken is wet, dip it back into the coating before frying. Fry the remaining pieces.

9 Rest the chicken for 3 minutes and enjoy with Honey Tabasco Sauce, Jalapeño Cornbread, and Coleslaw.

7

· SIDES ·

Our side dishes are great for sharing, perfect for
those guests who come into the restaurant and
want to try everything. They order three or four sides,
and then everyone is satisfied.

We have almost as many sides on the menu as entrées, which illustrates our attention to, say, the need for coleslaw with fried chicken, or onion rings with a burger, or cheese grits with your scrambled eggs. You can even make a whole meal out of our sides. This is especially true for vegetarians, who can still eat decadently at our restaurant, but within their zone.

We love the sides at Peter Luger — the hash browns, creamed spinach, and tomato-onion salad make the meal, and we were perhaps unconsciously inspired by that restaurant's philosophy. Neil has always loved a side of creamed spinach or coleslaw. I grew up loving all the side choices at Billy's on First Avenue, which has now closed but used to be the city's oldest restaurant (established in 1870), situated a stone's throw from my grandmother's front door. Billy's sides allowed you to build a great meal around a simple entrée you loved, and I suppose that's what you can do at the bakery today.

ONION *Rings*

SERVES 2 TO 3 (15 TO 18 RINGS) AS A SIDE DISH OR APPETIZER

1 *Vidalia onion*

2 CUPS *buttermilk*

4 TEASPOONS *salt, plus more for sprinkling*

1 TEASPOON *ground white pepper, plus more for sprinkling*

Canola or peanut oil

2 CUPS *all-purpose flour*

The longer these onions marinate, the more flavor they will have. One onion makes 15 to 18 rings. You may want to slice a second onion, as these rings will go fast!

1 Slice the onion into ½-inch-thick rings. Pop the outer rings into a large bowl. If the inner rings are too small for standard onion rings, keep them together for frying.

2 Whisk together the buttermilk, 2 teaspoons salt, and ½ teaspoon pepper, and pour the mixture over the onion rings. Allow the onions to marinate for at least 20 minutes and up to 24 hours in the fridge.

3 In a fryer or Dutch oven, heat the oil to 350°F. If the temperature is correct, the rings will take less time. Use a candy thermometer to get the best read. (If using a Dutch oven, fill it with 2 inches oil.) While the oil is heating, whisk together the flour with the remaining 2 teaspoons salt and ½ teaspoon pepper in a bowl.

4 Using a latex or disposable kitchen glove (tongs will break the onion rings), remove 2 to 3 rings at a time from the marinade and dip them into the flour mixture. Coat the rings and shake off the excess flour.

5 Fry 4 to 5 of the rings at a time (do not crowd them). Use a slotted spoon to push the rings down into the oil so that they continue to cook. Cook the rings for 3 to 5 minutes, or until golden brown. Remove with the slotted spoon. Place the rings onto a plate lined with a paper towel and immediately sprinkle them with salt and pepper to taste. Repeat the process until all the rings are cooked. Serve warm.

CREAMY *Cheese Grits*

SERVES 4

2 CUPS *whole milk*

PINCH *of cayenne pepper*

1 TEASPOON *salt*

½ TEASPOON *ground black pepper*

½ CUP *Quaker Quick Grits*

½ CUP *grated cheddar cheese*

½ CUP *grated Monterey Jack cheese*

....

RESTAURANT TRICK *If the grits become too thick, whisk in a little warm milk to thin them out.*

Grits may be a mystery north of the Mason-Dixon Line, but my father is from Atlanta — which means I grew up with grits on the breakfast table, and I've always recognized the draw of a savory morning porridge. As a kid, my brother would make Quaker Oats grits with shredded, prepackaged orange cheese, and it was damn good. Even if our taste buds weren't fully formed, we still appreciated the nutty texture of the grits. In 2005, after a visit with relatives in Georgia, I insisted that Neil start making cheese grits for brunch service. They soon became the base upon which our Southern Breakfast was built — a great foundation for a hearty plate of food. We also use grits for our dinner menu staple, Spicy Shrimp and Grits, and for our famous Baked Truffled Grits (page opposite).

1   Scald the milk (heat but do not boil) and seasonings in a heavy-bottomed saucepan on medium-high heat until the milk is hot to the touch and starts to foam around the sides but doesn't boil.

2   Whisk in the grits and cook on medium heat until smooth, about 8 to 10 minutes.

3   Remove the saucepan from the heat and stir in the cheeses. Check for seasoning and serve warm.

BAKED *Truffled Grits*

SERVES 2 TO 4

2 CUPS *whole milk*

½ CUP *dry instant grits*

½ CUP *shredded cheddar cheese*

½ CUP *shredded Monterey Jack cheese*

Salt to taste

Ground black pepper to taste

2 TABLESPOONS *canola or vegetable oil*

8 OUNCES *fresh mushrooms (oyster, shiitake, cremini, or any seasonal wild mushroom mix), stemmed and coarsely chopped*

2 TABLESPOONS *minced shallots*

1 TEASPOON *minced garlic*

1 TEASPOON *fresh thyme leaves, picked from stems*

1 CUP *shredded fontina cheese*

¼ CUP *breadcrumbs, preferably panko (Japanese breadcrumbs)*

1 TEASPOON *white truffle oil*

In January 2008, *Time Out New York* listed these grits as one of the finest dishes in the city. It's the perfect winter warmer, and a real show pony if you're looking to wow friends and family, or unfairly seduce your date. Although you can use extra virgin olive oil, the pure aroma of truffle oil is so intoxicating that it makes any dish special.

1 Bring the milk to a simmer in a 4-quart saucepan over medium-low heat. Slowly add the grits and stir with a wooden spoon until smooth, approximately 3 to 5 minutes. Turn off the heat and stir in cheddar and Monterey Jack. Stir the grits until the cheese melts, and the mixture is smooth and creamy. (If the grits get too thick, thin them out by stirring in a little water.) Season with salt and pepper, to taste. Pour the finished cheese grits into 4 buttered 10-ounce ramekins or a buttered 5-cup casserole.

2 Preheat a medium-sized sauté pan over medium-high heat and add the oil until smoking hot. Add the mushrooms and cook for 2 to 3 minutes until wilted and crispy on the edges.

3 Add the shallots, garlic, and thyme to the mushrooms and continue to sauté for 1 minute. Season with salt and pepper. Scatter the mushroom mixture over the grits and then top with the fontina and breadcrumbs.

4 Bake at 375°F for 12 to 15 minutes, or until the top is crusty and golden brown. Remove from the oven, drizzle with truffle oil, and serve immediately as a side dish or as a meal with a side salad.

FRIED GREEN *Tomatoes*

**SERVES 2 TO 4 AS AN
APPETIZER OR SIDE DISH**

ABOUT 5 *medium or large
green tomatoes (to yield ten
½-inch-thick slices)*

....

STATION 1

1 CUP *all-purpose flour*

1 TEASPOON *salt*

½ TEASPOON *cayenne pepper*

¼ TEASPOON *ground white pepper*

....

STATION 2

2 *large eggs*

2 TABLESPOONS *water*

PINCH *of salt*

....

STATION 3

1 CUP *panko breadcrumbs*

1 CUP *ground cornmeal*

PINCH *of salt*

....

½ CUP *canola oil*

Salt to taste

Green tomatoes are simply unripe, hard tomatoes. You'd think these babies would have no flavor or texture, but you'll see that once breaded, seasoned, and panfried, the green tomato morphs into an ethereal, juicy, sour, and succulent piece of fruit, with steaklike qualities. Any green tomato will do, whether it's a plum, beefsteak, or Roma. What matters here are the breadcrumbs. We use Japanese-style panko crumbs mixed with cornmeal, which lends this dish two different types of crispiness: the crunchy, nutty texture of the cornmeal when it fries, and the savory aspect of the panko when it crumbs (unlike the sandy texture you get from a traditional breadcrumb). To keep our tomatoes tinged with southern flavor, we season the flour with a little cayenne.

1   Slice the tomatoes into ½-inch-thick rounds. Line a cookie sheet with parchment paper or foil. Set up your three stations in sequence in shallow baking dishes or bowls. Use a whisk to combine each set of ingredients. If the cornmeal in Station 3 settles to the bottom, mix it with a whisk before coating each tomato slice. If the panko has large pieces, break them up with your fingers.

NOTE *The tomatoes should be standard or large size. They should be very green like tomatillos, but it's also okay if they have a little blush.*

RESTAURANT TRICK *The flour mixture seals the moisture in the tomatoes and creates a space between the tomato and the crispy, nongreasy panko and cornmeal coating. To make the coating process easier, glove one hand so that you always have a free and clean hand.*

You can tell if the oil has reached the perfect temperature by placing a small cube of bread in the pan. If it sizzles in the oil and browns quickly, the oil is ready for the tomatoes.

COMMON MISTAKE *Don't poke the tomatoes or shake the pan while they are frying (this will just make the tomatoes greasy). Use tongs to lift them by the sides when flipping them so that you don't remove the crust.*

2   Dredge the tomatoes in the flour mixture (Station 1), shake off the excess flour, and then dip them into the egg mixture (Station 2) until coated. Let any excess moisture drip off. Roll the tomatoes in the panko and cornmeal mixture (Station 3) until well coated. Place the tomatoes on the cookie sheet.

3   This recipe is very easily done without a deep fryer. In a 10- to 12-inch sauté pan, heat the oil over medium-high heat until it is just about to smoke. Sauté 3 to 4 tomato slices at a time for 1½ to 2 minutes total cooking time, flipping them halfway through. The tomatoes should be golden brown and crispy. Between batches, use a slotted spoon to lift out the brown crumbs. You can also transfer the top layer of oil to another sauté pan, leaving the crumbs and brown bits behind. The second and third batches may take a little longer because the oil will not be as hot.

4   Blot the fried tomatoes with paper towels and season with salt. Serve with Jalapeño Sour Cream (page 156) on the side.

COLESLAW

SERVES 4 TO 6 AS A SIDE DISH

8 CUPS *mixed shredded cabbage (6 cups green, 2 cups red)*

1 *medium carrot, julienned (or, to save time, use pre-julienned carrots)*

1 CUP *mayonnaise, such as Hellmann's or Best Foods*

½ CUP *sour cream*

¼ CUP *finely diced white or Vidalia onion*

1½ TABLESPOONS *sugar*

1 TABLESPOON *white wine vinegar*

¾ TABLESPOON *salt*

¼ TABLESPOON *ground black pepper*

....

NOTE *Make sure to remove the outer leaves of the cabbage, rinse the head well, and dry. Cut the cabbage in half and then into quarters, slicing through the fibrous core. Diagonally slice out the core in the center of the cabbage and discard, as it is too bitter to eat. To shred the cabbage using a knife, make sure to cut across the grain in even movements, creating thin slices. You can also use the grating tool on a food processor.*

I enjoy telling people that I married Neil for his coleslaw. It's not like I was always such a coleslaw lover, but Neil's sealed the deal. Not just a decoration on the plate or an afterthought, his slaw is hearty but elegant, slightly creamy, and has a nice balance of sweetness, acidity, and crunch. Plus I like that the vegetables don't get lost in a soupy mess.

As you might expect, Neil is a bit of a slaw fanatic and appreciates a good homemade version, whether vinegar-based, mayo-based, or made with something unconventional like celery root or jicama.

We use his coleslaw to accompany all of our sandwiches and burgers at the restaurant, and actually put it in our Real Turkey Sandwich (page 116), Jewish style, which pulls the whole thing together. For best results, allow this coleslaw to marinate, covered, in the fridge overnight. It gets better every day! You can make it with all green cabbage or all red, but we prefer a mix.

1   Combine the cabbage and the carrot.

2   In a bowl, whisk together the mayonnaise, sour cream, onion, sugar, vinegar, salt, and pepper. Add the dressing to the cabbage and carrots and mix both together with tongs or a spoon until well combined.

MEXICAN *Red Beans*

MAKES 2½ TO 3 CUPS

2 CUPS *dried red kidney beans*

½ CUP *chopped Spanish onion (half a medium onion)*

1 TEASPOON *chopped garlic (about 1 clove)*

½ CUP *chopped red bell pepper*

1 TABLESPOON *chopped fresh jalapeño pepper (or 1 small jalapeño)*

2 TABLESPOONS *extra virgin olive oil*

Salt and ground black pepper to taste

1 *bay leaf*

½ TEASPOON *dried oregano*

½ TEASPOON *ground cumin*

1 TEASPOON *chipotle peppers in adobo sauce*

½ CUP *chopped fresh cilantro*

1 Soak the beans in 4 cups cold water overnight in the refrigerator. Drain the beans.

2 In a large pot, sweat the onion, garlic, bell pepper, and jalapeño in 1 tablespoon of the olive oil with a pinch of salt and pepper.

3 Add the bay leaf, oregano, cumin, and chipotle.

4 Add the beans and 5 cups of water to the pot. Bring to a simmer and cook on low for 50 minutes.

5 Add cilantro and remaining olive oil and cook for another 10 minutes.

6 Remove the bay leaf. Season with salt and pepper and serve, or cool on an ice bath and refrigerate.

· THE ART OF THE ·
Potato

Plenty of men think of themselves as meat-and-potatoes guys, but Neil's an egg-and-potatoes guy. He believes that no egg dish should go without a great potato accompaniment. A fan of old-school diners in Brooklyn, he's sat at a great many counters watching potatoes get ruined. He's learned that charming antique diner griddles do not augur well for a potato's success; they produced potatoes that were never crisp enough on the outside, or if they were, it was at the expense of moistness inside.

We make our hash browns almost like a cake, with a crusty outside around a nice and creamy middle. You never get this from an old diner griddle because that dual texture comes only from a pan. This is lucky for home cooks.

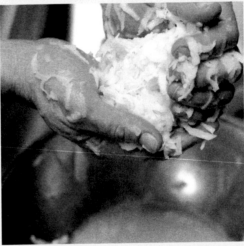

The best method for breakfast potatoes is to use day-old baked potatoes, never frozen, and delicious clarified butter (page 143). We actually use clarified butter in concert with canola oil. Together they sing without making the potatoes too greasy.

At Community Food & Juice, we add carrot to the hash for a health food note. You can do the same; toss an additional ingredient — mushrooms, onions, or any other vegetable — in with the potato mix, which will form a nice crust.

POTATO *Pancakes*

MAKES 4 SERVINGS (2 TO 3 PANCAKES PER PERSON)

4 large Idaho potatoes

Juice of half a lemon

2 large eggs

½ CUP finely minced or grated onion (about half a medium onion)

1 ½ TEASPOONS salt

¼ TEASPOON ground white pepper

4 TABLESPOONS all-purpose flour (substitute matzo meal if you don't want to use flour)

¼ TO ½ CUP canola oil

....

NOTE *The added potato starch makes the pancakes crispy.*

We prefer to finely mince the onion by hand because grating the onion creates a lot of water.

If you want to reheat the pancakes, place them on a cookie sheet and warm them in the oven at 350°F for up to 10 minutes until they recrisp, but be careful — they dry out easily.

Those of us who grew up in a Jewish family undoubtedly remember a mother, an aunt, or an in-law serving soggy gray potato pancakes for Hanukkah. Not crispy, not golden, undercooked in the middle.

Many older cooks insist that draining their pancakes on brown paper bags is the secret to making them great, but aside from the right frying technique, the key actually rests in the potato starch, which must be squeezed out during prep and added back later. When the starch rejoins its family of potatoes, they will cook off with a crispy, crunchy exterior and a divine potato flavor. Not to mention that each pancake will be certifiably, deliciously, golden brown. These pancakes go wonderfully with our Cinnamon Sour Cream (page 157).

1   Peel the potatoes and place them in a bowl of cold water.

2   Grate the potatoes on the medium or largest holes of a box grater and into a clean bowl (or use the shredding tool of a food processor).

3   Squeeze the lemon juice over the potatoes and mix it in with your hands (to keep the potatoes from browning).

4   Using your hands, squeeze the liquid from the shredded potatoes into another bowl and reserve (see page 136).

5   In a clean bowl, add the eggs, onion, salt, and pepper to the dry shredded potato mixture. Mix in the flour until combined.

6   Discard the top layer of the reserved potato liquid and save the sludgy starch at the bottom of the bowl. Add the starch back into the potato mixture and mix in with your hands or a spoon.

7   In a large sauté pan, heat the canola oil to just below the smoking point. Form eight to twelve 2-inch pancakes. Sauté four pancakes at a time, making sure that the oil coats them. (You can flatten them with your spatula if you prefer a thinner pancake.) Once a pancake has golden edges and is partially cooked in the middle, the pancake is ready to be turned. When flipping a pancake, tilt the pan away from you so that the oil doesn't spray and burn you. Lower the heat so that the pancakes will continue to cook through and won't burn before they're done cooking, about another 3 to 4 minutes. When done, remove the pancakes from the pan and place them on a paper-towel-lined plate.

8   Before cooking the remaining pancakes, remove the excess potato pieces from the pan with a paper towel or spoon.

9   Serve the pancakes warm or at room temperature, perhaps with Cinnamon Sour Cream (page 157) and our Homemade Caramelized Applesauce (page 151).

POTATO & CELERY ROOT *Pancakes*

**MAKES 4 TO 5 SERVINGS
(2 PANCAKES PER PERSON)**

4 *medium Idaho potatoes, peeled*

Juice of half a lemon

1 *small celery root, about ¾ pound*

2 *large eggs*

½ CUP *finely minced or grated onion
(about half a medium onion)*

1½ TEASPOONS *salt*

¼ TEASPOON *ground white pepper*

6 TABLESPOONS *all-purpose flour*

¼ TO ½ CUP *canola oil*

....

NOTE *The added potato starch
makes the pancakes crispy.*

*The pancakes go well with Home-
made Caramelized Applesauce (page
151) or alongside a pot roast or pork
roast. The celery root makes these
potato pancakes different by giving
them a nice kick.*

This is the version we serve at Community Food & Juice, our restaurant uptown.
It's a little twist on a great classic.

1   Grate the peeled potatoes on the medium or largest holes of a box grater
into a bowl (or use the shredding tool on a food processor).

2   Squeeze the lemon juice over the potatoes and mix it in with your hands.

3   Using your hands, squeeze the liquid from the shredded potatoes into
another bowl and reserve.

4   Remove both ends of the celery root. Peel the skin with a knife, as you
would remove the skin of a butternut squash. Grate the celery root as you did
the potatoes, add to the shredded potatoes, and combine.

5   In a clean bowl, mix the eggs, onion, salt, and pepper. Add the egg mixture
to the shredded potato mixture. Mix in the flour until combined.

6   Discard the top layer of the reserved potato liquid and save the starch at
the bottom of the bowl. Add the starch back into the potato mixture and mix in
with your hands or a spoon.

7   In a large sauté pan, heat the canola oil to just below the smoking point.
With your hands, form eight to ten 4-inch pancakes. Sauté four pancakes at a
time, making sure that the oil coats the pancakes. (You can flatten them with
your spatula if you prefer a thinner pancake.) Once a pancake has golden edges
and is partially cooked in the middle, the pancake is ready to be turned. When
flipping a pancake, tilt the pan away from you so that the oil doesn't spray and
burn you. Lower the heat so that the pancakes will continue to cook through
and won't burn before they're done cooking, about another 3 to 4 minutes.
When done, remove the pancakes from the pan and place them on a paper-
towel-lined plate.

8   Before cooking the remaining pancakes, remove the excess pieces from the
pan with a paper towel or spoon.

RED FLANNEL *Hash*

SERVES 5 TO 6

2 POUNDS *cooked corned beef brisket*

1 TABLESPOON *plus* 1 TEASPOON *extra virgin olive oil*

2 CUPS *Idaho potatoes, cut into ¼-inch dice*

1 *medium carrot, cut into ¼-inch dice*

HALF *a medium Spanish onion, cut into ¼-inch dice*

1 TABLESPOON *thyme leaves*

1 TEASPOON *salt*

¼ TEASPOON *ground white pepper*

2 *medium cooked beets, cut into ¼-inch dice*

2 TABLESPOONS *unsalted butter*

2 TABLESPOONS *canola oil*

This hash is called Red Flannel because the combination of the beets and vegetables makes it look like a plaid shirt. At least that's Neil's thinking.

1 Preheat the oven to 325°F.

2 Using a food processor, pulverize 1 pound of the corned beef until it reaches a mousselike texture. Chop the remaining pound of corned beef into ¼-inch dice. Add both to the same bowl.

3 Oil a cookie sheet with 1 teaspoon of olive oil. Place the potatoes, carrot, and onion on the sheet. Use your hands to mix together the vegetables with the remaining 1 tablespoon olive oil and the thyme, salt, and pepper and spread them evenly on the sheet. Roast for 15 minutes, until the vegetables have a little color but are tender and cooked through. Halfway through the roasting process, stir the vegetables so that they do not brown or form a crust. Allow them to cool.

4 Add the cooled vegetables and beets to the bowl of corned beef. Using clean or gloved hands, mix the ingredients together until well combined and the ingredients are evenly dispersed among the mixture.

5 Put a 12-by-15-inch sheet of parchment on your countertop. Press the mixture onto the sheet. Make sure that the hash is compacted so it is thick and dense. Use an empty tuna can or 3-inch biscuit cutter to punch out patties that are 3 inches in diameter and 1½ inches high. If the patties don't seem thick enough, use extra scraps and compact the scraps on top of the patties in the biscuit cutter or tuna can. You should be able to make 10 to 12 patties. Transfer them to a parchment- or foil-lined cookie sheet.

6 Raise the oven temperature to 350°F. In a large nonstick sauté pan, heat 1 tablespoon of the butter and 1 tablespoon of the canola oil over medium heat until the butter is melted and the oil is hot. Re-form the patties with your hands before laying 4 at a time into the sauté pan. Sauté them 2 to 3 minutes, until golden brown. Use a spatula to flip them and sauté the patties for 2 more minutes and place them on a cookie sheet. Repeat the process with the remaining patties. Cook them in the oven for 3 to 4 minutes, until cooked all the way through.

7 Serve with eggs any style, including poached eggs with Hollandaise Sauce (page 58).

HASH BROWNS

SERVES 4

4 *Idaho, russet, or Yukon gold potatoes (or any large and seasonal varieties)*

3 TABLESPOONS *clarified butter (see below)*

3 TABLESPOONS *canola oil*

Kosher salt
Freshly ground white pepper, to taste

....

NOTE *Be sure to use an old omelet or fry pan that is highly seasoned, or try a well-used Teflon pan. The roundness of the pan makes the cake cook evenly.*

RESTAURANT TRICK *It's helpful to have a premade salt-and-pepper mix on hand. We prepare a dozen 1-quart containers a week filled with three parts kosher salt to one part ground white pepper. (Ideally you should grind the fresh white peppercorns yourself in a pepper mill or coffee or spice grinder.)*

COMMON MISTAKE *Don't chop the potatoes or touch or turn them in the pan. This will make them absorb more of the oil and render them too greasy.*

The greatest hash browns are made from twice-cooked potatoes, in a round seasoned pan, over medium-high heat. The trick is to let the pan and potatoes do the work. At the bakery, we cook our hash browns, big two-inch-thick potato cakes, in individual fry pans. This method makes them crispy brown on both sides, with a steamy, creamy, chunky middle. For service, we spoon out heaping portions of these hash-brown cakes—the perfect accompaniment to our eggs and biscuit sandwiches. Even though we call them hash browns they can translate into a great dinner potato with a piece of seared fish, a great steak, even roasted chicken.

1   Preheat the oven to 350°F. Bake the potatoes for 50 minutes, or until mostly cooked through. Let cool.

2   With a small paring knife, shave off the ends and peel the skins. Push the peeled, cooked potato through a screen (for cooling cake) or cooling rack, so that you have long sticks or pieces of cooked potato that resemble a lumpy mash.

3   Warm a fry pan over medium-high heat for 1 to 2 minutes, until hot. Then add 2 tablespoons of the clarified butter and 2 tablespoons of the canola oil, until slightly smoking.

4   Add all the potato to the pan and let it cook until a crunchy outside forms. Sprinkle with salt and pepper. Flip the cake once with a spatula and let sit for 1 to 2 minutes, letting the heat of the pan do the work. Drizzle the remaining butter and oil around the edges of the potato cake, to keep it crispy brown. Peek underneath with a spatula. When the cake is golden brown, remove the pan from the heat. Adjust the seasoning to taste.

....

HOW TO MAKE CLARIFIED BUTTER

Clarified butter is simply unsalted butter with its milk solids and water removed, so that the butterfat remains. (Clarified butter is great for making crispy hash browns because of its high smoke point and ability to fry without burning.)

1 stick (8 tablespoons) unsalted butter

In a saucepan, gently melt the butter over low heat until three layers form (if you've ever left a dish of butter out too long in the sun, you know exactly how this looks). Skim off the top white foamy layer with a spoon. When all the white foam has been skimmed and the milky layer on the bottom of the pan has stopped bubbling, remove the saucepan from the heat. Let the butter sit for a few minutes to allow the milk solids to settle further to the bottom. Then strain the mixture through a fine sieve or a cheesecloth-lined strainer. The rich golden yellow liquid you've retained is the clarified butter. Keeps several months in the refrigerator, covered.

GRILLED WILD MUSHROOM
Goat Cheese Pizzas

Pizza Dough (recipe below)

¾ CUP *Caramelized Onions (page 114)*

1½ CUPS *Wild Mushroom Mix (page 146)*

8 OUNCES *goat cheese, soft and creamy*

2 TO 3 OUNCES *truffle oil*

Salt

Ground black pepper

In autumn and winter, we serve these pizzas as hors d'oeuvres at our catered events because they're easy to eat, slightly sophisticated, and wholly satisfying. The dough comes together very easily and the flavor is a wonderful balance of earthy, woodsy, creamy sweetness.

1   Place an oven rack in the middle of the oven and preheat to 400°F.

2   Top each pizza with 2 tablespoons Caramelized Onions, spreading the onions as you would a tomato sauce. Top with 3 tablespoons Wild Mushroom Mix. Dot with 2 tablespoons goat cheese. Drizzle each pizza with 1 teaspoon truffle oil and sprinkle on salt and pepper.

3   Grill each individual pizza on a hot grill or griddle until grill marks appear and the texture of the dough is like that of pita bread. The surface will begin to bubble and blister.

4   Carefully remove the pizzas from the grill or griddle and place them directly on the middle oven rack with no sheet pan. If you are worried about drippings, put a sheet pan directly under the pizzas in the rack below. Bake for 5 to 7 minutes, until the crust is crisp and the goat cheese has melted.

5   Drizzle with more truffle oil, cut into wedges, and serve hot.

2 TABLESPOONS *extra virgin olive oil*

1 TABLESPOON *light brown sugar*

1 TEASPOON *active dry yeast*

½ TEASPOON *salt*

¾ TEASPOON *fresh rosemary leaves, chopped*

1 *small clove garlic, chopped*

4 CUPS *(1 pound) bread flour or all-purpose flour*

Pizza Dough

1   Combine 1 tablespoon of the olive oil with the sugar, yeast, salt, rosemary, garlic, and 1½ cups warm water in the bowl of a standing mixer. Mix together the ingredients with the bread hook on low speed. Add the flour all at once and mix on low for 2 to 3 minutes, until the dough sticks to the bread hook and is smooth and elastic. If you do not have a standing mixer, you can use a large bowl and stir with a wooden spoon.

2   Coat the bottom and sides of a large stainless-steel or ceramic bowl with the remaining tablespoon olive oil. Transfer the dough from the mixing bowl to the oil-coated bowl. Use your hands to flip the dough in the bowl so that it is evenly coated in oil. Cover the bowl with plastic wrap or a moist kitchen towel and put it in a warm place. Allow the dough to double in volume, which will take about 1 hour.

(continued on page 146)

3 When the dough has risen, remove it from the bowl and portion it by cutting the dough in half, then slicing each half into thirds. Each piece will weigh about 5 ounces.

4 Lightly flour a cutting board. Place one piece of the dough on the board and use your fingers to stretch the dough into an 8- to 9-inch circle with a rounded border for the pizza crust. Repeat with the remaining 5 pieces.

2 CUPS *field or button mushrooms, rinsed, patted dry, and sliced*

1 CUP *shiitake mushrooms, stemmed and cut into thick strips*

1 CUP *oyster mushrooms, stemmed and cut into large chunks*

2 TABLESPOONS *extra virgin olive oil*

1 CLOVE *garlic, chopped*

2 TEASPOONS *chopped fresh rosemary or thyme leaves*

1 TEASPOON *salt*

¼ TEASPOON *ground white pepper*

Wild Mushroom Mix

1 Preheat the oven to 375°F.

2 Combine all of the ingredients together in a bowl until the mushrooms are well coated with the seasonings and oil.

3 Roast on a sheet pan for 15 minutes, until the mushrooms are browned and caramelized. Be careful not to burn the garlic. Let the mushrooms cool.

SUGAR-CURED *Bacon*

SERVES 4

12 SLICES *double-cut sliced bacon (preferably nitrate-free)*

1 CUP *sugar (go organic if it'll make you feel better)*

....

NOTE *Heat up the bacon later if desired by warming it in a 350°F oven for 2 to 3 minutes. Serve it right out of the pan with eggs any style, some grits with a little cheese, and fried green tomatoes, and you've got our Southern Breakfast (page 53).*

Regular breakfast bacon is too thin for this recipe because it cooks up too crispy and brittle. You need something thick enough to sustain the sugar. If you don't see prepackaged thick-sliced bacon at your grocery store, ask for it at the meat counter or visit your local butcher.

Back when I was switching from a career in editing magazine pages to a life in food, I volunteered at the New School's Culinary Arts Program, which used to be in Greenwich Village. We worked on a barter system; I traded hours of prepping, cleaning, and assisting for free classes — and even better, free tasting.

At the time, I lived in a shoebox studio apartment on Jane Street. The school was so close to my apartment that if my call time was 1:45, I could leave at 1:44, dart across Greenwich Avenue, and still arrive with seconds to spare.

My favorite teacher there was Carmen Cook, from Iowa. Her specialty was something she called sugar-cured bacon. It was so delicious, so sinful, so sensuous, that it made one guilty vegetarian in the class go carnivore the second its fatty, decadent aroma wafted through the room.

The bacon couldn't have been easier to make. With thick, strong arms, Carmen liberally sprinkled sheet pans of double-cut sliced bacon with a blanket of white granulated sugar. ("Yes, you need that much sugar to get it right.") She shoved the trays in the oven, and twenty minutes later we all died and went to pig heaven.

When the brunch craze started to spike at the bakery, I remembered Carmen's recipe and asked Neil to put it on the menu. We're told some loyalists wait hours in line just for this side dish.

1   Preheat the oven to 350°F.

2   Cover the bottom of a sheet pan with parchment paper or aluminum foil and lay the bacon strips out on the pan, making sure to separate every strip. Take a handful of sugar and generously dust it on top of each slice so that every inch is covered (Carmen did it straight from the box). Bake it in the oven for 20 to 27 minutes.

3   After 10 to 12 minutes, check on the bacon to make sure it isn't burning. Eventually, the sugar will caramelize with the fat and become crunchy. When the bacon is crisp on the bottom and the sugar coating has made a nice shiny top, pull the strips off the pan with tongs and blot them with paper towels while hot. (Do not drain on paper towels as the paper will stick, but a cloth towel works.)

GRANOLA

MAKES 5 CUPS

2½ CUPS *Quaker Quick Oats or any brand 5-minute oats*

½ CUP *sliced almonds*

½ CUP *unsalted cashews or pecan halves and pieces*

½ TEASPOON *cinnamon*

¼ TEASPOON *nutmeg (ground or freshly grated)*

PINCH *of salt*

1 STICK (8 TABLESPOONS) *unsalted butter*

⅓ CUP *maple syrup*

⅓ CUP *light brown sugar*

¾ TEASPOON *orange extract (substitute orange zest if you can't find orange extract)*

1 CUP *mixed dried fruit*

....

NOTE *Use any combination of dried fruit you desire — be as creative as you like! Shredded coconut (2 tablespoons) is a good addition.*

Almonds are the mainstay in this granola, but you can substitute any other nuts for the cashews. We like the cashews for their richness.

If you like granola very toasted or roasted or like the nuts well done, bake it a little longer — but be careful not to burn it. If you like your granola blonder and less crunchy, bake it 5 minutes less than recommended here. This is a very forgiving recipe. Slip on your Birkenstocks and enjoy.

1 Preheat the oven to 350°F.

2 In a large bowl, whisk together the oats, nuts, spices, and salt until combined.

3 Over low heat in a medium saucepan, whisk together the butter, syrup, sugar, and extract until the sugar has dissolved and the butter has melted.

4 Pour the wet ingredients over the dry ingredients and mix thoroughly.

5 Line a cookie sheet with parchment paper. Coat the edges of the sheet with nonstick spray so that the granola does not burn. If parchment paper is unavailable, spray the entire cookie sheet. Spread the granola on the sheet lightly and evenly.

6 Bake until golden brown, approximately 20 to 22 minutes. Rotate the cookie sheet in the oven halfway through the cooking time to ensure even baking.

7 Remove the sheet from the oven and allow the granola to cool. Chop the dried fruit into 1/4-inch dice. Break up the granola by hand and add the dried fruit. Store in a tightly sealed container. The granola will be good for 2 to 3 months if stored in a cool, dark spot with low humidity.

HOMEMADE CARAMELIZED *Applesauce*

**MAKES 4 SERVINGS
(2 TO 2½ CUPS)**

6 *medium Granny Smith apples*

1 CUP *sugar*

2 *cinnamon sticks*

2 TABLESPOONS *unsalted butter*

1 TEASPOON *vanilla extract*

Zest of 1 lemon (1 to 2 tablespoons)

Juice of 1 lemon

....

NOTE *The applesauce will keep for up to 2 weeks in the fridge in a covered jar. At home, we spoon it into hot oatmeal for a delicious breakfast treat.*

Once you taste our applesauce, you'll never go back to the bland, yellow store-bought stuff. For the best sauce, be discriminating about your apples. If they're too sweet — for instance, a Delicious, Fuji, or Jonagold — your sauce may turn out, well, too sweet. Granny Smiths are excellent because they impart a tartness to the sauce and balance out the sugar, vanilla, butter, and cinnamon. Of course, local varietal apples are the best: ask your farmer for a hard, tart, cooking variety, and you will be sure to have a chunky, rich sauce.

1   Peel and core the apples. Cut them into 2-inch chunks. Place the apples in a heavy-bottomed saucepan. Add the remaining ingredients. The sugar will dissolve when heated.

2   Over medium-high heat, bring to a boil. The apples will fall apart and the ingredients will start to melt into a thick apple soup. Cook down over high heat, about 30 to 40 minutes. Do not stir until the water has evaporated and the sugar turns into a brown film, caramelizing on the bottom of the pan (see photo). This caramelization is your indication to lower the flame to medium-low. Now stir and turn over the apples a few times to create a new crust.

3   Each time the bottom of the pan becomes caramelized, stir the sauce. Continue to use a spoon (wooden is best) to break up the apples.

4   The applesauce is done when the apples are cooked through and little chunks remain. The sauce will be a deep caramel color. This will take about another 25 to 30 minutes.

5   Remove the cinnamon sticks before serving, or keep them in for a rustic look.

8

CONDIMENTS .

Many of the dishes on our menu are simple and
straightforward, but the condiments are what make
them stand out. What's a Buttermilk Biscuit Sandwich
without delectable Tomato Jam to give it that one-two
punch of acidity and sweetness? Huevos Rancheros
would be a yawn without Jalapeño Sour Cream to wake
it up with a bright, fresh zing.

The best thing about condiments is that you can use them with other dishes. Take the
Tomatillo Sauce (page 165): it's a classic Mexican green sauce that can be used not only with
eggs, but also with grilled chicken, pulled pork, even as a topping on roasted or fried fish. The
Tartar Sauce — perfect on a crispy fish Po' Boy — can easily be turned into Russian dressing
for our Real Turkey Sandwich just by adding a few spoonfuls of ketchup. And the fresh Raspberry Jam obviously goes well with muffins and biscuits, but on Jalapeño Cornbread (page
45) it creates a marriage of savory, hot, and sweet that could make you blush.

We're obviously biased, but we think there's no substitute for a homemade condiment.
Luckily, amateur cooks and condiments go together like bread and butter. If you don't yet
know your way around the kitchen, start with condiments. In truth, you're concocting
(without much cooking) the ingredients — the secret is that all you need is a food processor,
a whisk, and a bowl.

GUACAMOLE

4 *Hass avocados, soft to the touch but not mushy*

2 TABLESPOONS *lime juice*

3 TABLESPOONS *minced red onion*

3 TABLESPOONS *minced fresh jalapeño pepper (including seeds)*

2 TEASPOONS *salt, preferably kosher*

¼ TO ½ TEASPOON *ground black pepper*

¼ CUP *fresh cilantro leaves, loosely packed*

....

TRY THIS *Use a garlic press to mince the jalapeño, and wear gloves while handling it to avoid a burn.*

Here's a trick you might not know: When storing guacamole, pour 1 tablespoon canola or olive oil on top to prevent discoloration. Seal the bowl in plastic wrap.

1   Halve the avocados lengthwise and remove the pits, reserving two. Scoop the flesh into a bowl with a large tablespoon, scraping out any remaining pieces. Discard the skins.

2   Add the lime juice to the bowl. Using a potato masher or sturdy whisk, mash the avocado with the juice until the mixture is somewhat chunky but pureed and pulverized in parts. Mix in the onion, jalapeño, and salt and pepper with a spoon.

3   Chop the cilantro leaves and add them to the guacamole. Adjust the seasoning to taste.

4   Serve with a bowl of tortilla chips with the pits inserted for a rustic touch. They will also keep the avocado from turning brown.

JALAPEÑO *Sour Cream*

MAKES 2½ CUPS

¾ CUP *fresh cilantro leaves, tightly packed*

¼ CUP *fresh lime juice*

1½ TABLESPOONS *minced fresh jalapeño pepper (seeds included)*

1 CLOVE *garlic, finely minced*

2 TEASPOONS *salt*

¼ TEASPOON *ground white pepper*

2 CUPS *sour cream*

....

TRY THIS *Use a garlic press to mince the jalapeño, and wear gloves while handling it to avoid a burn.*

This recipe is great with Mexican cuisine or anything that calls for a bright, sharp, and creamy sauce. It tastes especially delicious with tortilla chips, enchiladas, and nachos. At Clinton St., we use it as a topping for our fish tacos, as a side dipping sauce for our Fried Green Tomatoes (page 132), or to top our Huevos Rancheros (page 54).

1   With the blender on medium speed, blend together the first 6 ingredients until well combined.

2   Turn off the blender and add the sour cream. To combine the ingredients, start the blender on low. As the ingredients gradually come together, you can raise the speed of the blender. Adjust the seasoning to taste.

3   The Jalapeño Sour Cream will keep for 1 week to 10 days in the fridge.

HONEY *Tabasco Sauce*

MAKES ½ CUP

½ CUP *honey*

1 TEASPOON *Tabasco sauce*

....

NOTE *If you prefer a spicier sauce, add additional dashes of Tabasco.*

Honey Tabasco Sauce resulted from one of those happy accidents on the plate. It was the late eighties, and Neil and his former wife, Sonia, were at a restaurant with friends, enjoying bar food. Neil was dipping fried chicken wings in honey, and Sonia accidentally doused one with hot sauce before taking a dip. *Ahí lo tienes!* A new favorite condiment and family food tradition was born.

Mix the honey and Tabasco together with a spoon. Serve at room temperature or warm. Store this mixture in the fridge. If you need to warm it quickly, microwave for 10 to 15 seconds on high heat.

CINNAMON *Sour Cream*

MAKES 1 CUP

1 CUP *sour cream (low-fat is okay)*

2 TABLESPOONS *cinnamon sugar (2 tablespoons sugar and ¼ teaspoon ground cinnamon)*

Use this sour cream as an extra special garnish on our Potato Pancakes (page 138) or with our Vanilla Buttermilk Waffles (page 87).

Mix all ingredients together until well blended.

HERB *Mayo*

MAKES 1 CUP

½ CUP *fresh basil leaves*

½ CUP *fresh parsley leaves*

½ CUP *minced fresh chives*

2 TABLESPOONS *fresh thyme leaves*

1 CUP *mayonnaise, such as Hellmann's or Best Foods*

1 TEASPOON *freshly squeezed lemon juice*

½ TEASPOON *salt*

¼ TEASPOON *ground white pepper*

....

NOTE *You must mince the chives ahead of time because if left whole they will shred in the food processor.*

RESTAURANT TRICK *When removing the mayonnaise from the food processor, pull out the blade and scrape it as best you can. Place it back in the bowl, cover, and pulse once more. The blade will spin off any excess mayonnaise. Pull out the blade again and scrape the sides.*

1   Pulse together the herbs in a food processor until they are finely chopped and resemble a paste.

2   Add the mayonnaise, lemon juice, and salt and pepper. Blend together until the mayonnaise is bright green. The Herb Mayo will remain fresh in a tightly sealed container in the fridge for 1 to 2 weeks.

CAJUN *Remoulade*

MAKES 3 CUPS

¼ CUP *tarragon vinegar*

2 TABLESPOONS *freshly squeezed lemon juice*

2 TABLESPOONS *Creole mustard*

1 TEASPOON *paprika*

½ TEASPOON *cayenne pepper*

1 TABLESPOON *salt*

¼ TABLESPOON *ground white pepper*

½ CUP *extra virgin olive oil*

½ CUP *canola oil*

⅔ CUP *minced scallions (white and green parts)*

1 LARGE STALK *celery, minced*

¼ CUP *finely diced fennel bulb*

¼ CUP *minced fresh parsley*

1 CUP *mayonnaise, such as Hellmann's or Best Foods*

....

NOTE *The remoulade will stay fresh for 3 to 4 weeks if stored in the fridge in a tightly sealed container.*

Creole mustard can be found at specialty gourmet food stores. If you can't find it, try Pommery or seeded mustard with the addition of a teaspoon of any type of vinegar, preferably red (but not balsamic).

Our remoulade is a piquant sauce that has a kick to it. Serve it with crab cakes, fried fish, or Fried Green Tomatoes. This sauce also goes well with boiled shrimp or any sort of seafood cocktail.

1   Whisk together the tarragon vinegar, lemon juice, mustard, paprika, cayenne, salt, and pepper in a bowl.

2   Slowly pour the extra virgin olive and canola oils in a steady stream into the mixture, whisking continuously. Stir in the vegetables, parsley, and the mayonnaise. Whisk until smooth and all of the ingredients are well incorporated. Adjust the seasoning to taste if necessary.

RASPBERRY *Jam*

MAKES 2 CUPS

3 CUPS *fresh or frozen raspberries (or blueberries, strawberries, blackberries, etc.)*

2 CUPS *sugar*

¼ CUP *freshly squeezed lemon juice*

1 TABLESPOON *quick-set pectin*

....

NOTE *If you want a thicker jam and do not have pectin, you can always cook the jam down further over low heat until it's thick enough. However, pectin is what adds shelf life to jams. If you make it without pectin, eat it fast!*

There's nothing worse than spreading gummy commercial jam on your hot buttermilk biscuit, fresh from the oven. Neil decided we had to make our own. He started with varying seasonal fruits, from strawberry to mixed forest berry to apricot and orange, but raspberry has always been the hands-down favorite. If you prefer another flavor, substitute any fruit you like.

1   In a 4-quart heavy-bottomed pot, mix together the berries, sugar, lemon juice, and pectin. Bring to a boil while stirring over medium-high heat (3 to 5 minutes). The sugar will dissolve to create a loose, saucy consistency. Turn down the heat to low and simmer, stirring occasionally, until the jam thickens, 15 to 20 minutes. Scrape the bottom of the pot periodically to prevent sticking.

2   Turn off the heat and let the jam cool at room temperature or put the pot in an ice bath for quicker results, stirring until the jam is cool. Transfer to a crock, a jam jar, or even a bowl. This jam thickens as it cools and keeps at least 3 weeks in the refrigerator.

TOMATO *Jam*

MAKES 2 CUPS

¼ CUP *extra virgin olive oil*

HALF *a Spanish onion, finely diced*

4 CLOVES *garlic, minced*

2 SPRIGS *fresh rosemary, finely chopped*

PINCH *of red pepper flakes*

4 CUPS *(approximately 8 to 10) peeled, seeded, and roughly chopped plum tomatoes*

Salt

Ground black pepper

....

NOTE *To peel and seed tomatoes, bring a pot of water to boil. On the bottom of each tomato (the end without the core), make a shallow "X" with your knife. Boil each tomato for 15 to 30 seconds, until the skin starts to curl away from the "X." Remove the tomato from the boiling water and shock it in ice water for about 15 seconds. When the tomato is cool enough to handle, peel away the skin and discard. Slice each tomato in half vertically and, using a spoon or your fingers, pull out and discard the seeds. The tomatoes are now ready to be roughly chopped for the jam.*

Tomato Jam is a fancy ketchup or a thick marinara in disguise. It makes any old burger special, but it was tailor made for our Buttermilk Biscuit Sandwiches (page 18) and serves as the perfect savory complement to the eggs, cheese, and biscuit. It can also be used in an omelet, or mixed in with a baked pasta, like ziti. Or just keep it on hand as your favorite designer condiment.

1   In a heavy-bottomed saucepan, warm ⅛ cup of the olive oil. Sauté the onion, garlic, rosemary, and red pepper flakes over medium-high heat until the mixture is tender but not brown.

2   Once the mixture has softened, add the chopped tomatoes and reduce the heat to medium. Continue to cook until the tomatoes have given up most of their moisture and turned a deep orange-red, making sure to stir often, 15 to 20 minutes.

3   Season the jam with salt and pepper and finish with the remaining olive oil.

TARTAR *Sauce*

MAKES 2 CUPS

½ **CUP** *coarsely chopped sour pickles (ours come from the Pickle Guys on the Lower East Side)*

¼ **CUP** *drained, coarsely chopped capers*

¼ **CUP** *yellow onion, finely diced*

2 **TABLESPOONS** *coarsely chopped fresh parsley*

1½ **CUPS** *mayonnaise, such as Hellmann's or Best Foods*

Juice of half a lemon

1 **TEASPOON** *Tabasco sauce*

1 **TEASPOON** *Worcestershire sauce*

Salt and ground black pepper

Tartar Sauce is the classic accompaniment to fried fish. It's crunchy, tart, savory, and creamy. Serve this with the Po' Boy (page 108) or any fried, broiled, or seared fish. This sauce also goes well with fish and chips and can be used as a base for deli-style Russian dressing.

1   Combine the pickles, capers, onion, and parsley in a bowl.

2   Whisk in the mayonnaise, lemon juice, and Tabasco and Worcestershire sauces until well combined. Season to taste with salt and pepper.

TOMATILLO *Sauce*

MAKES 2 CUPS

4 CUPS *husked tomatillos (4 to 6 medium or 8 to 10 small), quartered or chopped*

HALF *a large white onion, cut into chunks (same size as tomatillo pieces)*

4 TO 5 CLOVES *garlic*

1 *medium fresh jalapeño pepper, chopped*

2 TABLESPOONS *extra virgin olive oil*

1½ TEASPOONS *salt*

½ TEASPOON *ground black pepper*

½ CUP *fresh cilantro leaves, tightly packed*

....

COMMON MISTAKE *It's important to make sure the roasted ingredients are cool when you add them to the food processor for blending, so the cilantro will keep its color and stay green. If the ingredients are hot when you add the fresh herbs, the tomatillo sauce will turn a murky and unappetizing green.*

NOTE *You can adjust the heat of the sauce to your liking with the jalapeño. Tomatillo sauce is traditionally tart and sweet with heat. If you like your sauce less hot, use half a jalapeño or remove the seeds from a whole jalapeño before roasting.*

1 Preheat the oven to 375°F.

2 Gently toss together the tomatillos, onion, garlic, and jalapeño with the oil, salt, and pepper so that every vegetable is well coated on a sheet pan or cookie sheet. Spread the mixture out evenly on the pan.

3 Roast the ingredients for 10 to 15 minutes, until softened. Cool for 10 minutes.

4 Once cool, scrape all the vegetables and juice into the bowl of a food processor. Pulse 4 to 5 times, until the ingredients resemble a coarse chop. Add the cilantro and pulse until the sauce is pureed and the cilantro is incorporated into the sauce.

5 Adjust the seasoning with salt and pepper to taste.

9

. DESSERT .

....

The secret to our desserts is that we're a small bakeshop. When we sell out of something, it's gone until it's made fresh the next day. The cookies are baked every morning. And our ice cream — handcrafted by one man expressly for us — is delivered from Brooklyn every week.

....

Unlike large retail stores or supermarkets, we don't have freezers full of cakes waiting to be frosted, or presliced portions matted between cardboard. Our bakers use their hands to fold dough and sprinkle sugar. They brush butter and bake batter in the early hours of the morning. They work with organic cage-free eggs; they cut chunks from Valrhona chocolate; they squeeze the juice from tiny Key limes. In short, they handcraft every dessert we sell, from the peanut brittle that tops our parfaits to the lemon curd filling our cakes.

You don't have to be the best baker in the world to make something memorable. The first cake I ever made from scratch was Mollie Katzen's all-butter pound cake from the *Moosewood Cookbook*. I spent nine dollars at Balducci's on the fanciest, finest French hotel butter I could find. I bought organic cane sugar and organic flour, farmers'-market brown eggs, organic vanilla extract, and grass-fed cow's milk. This cake must have cost thirty dollars to make. It tasted like a million bucks. Baking seasonally is another safe idea, when fruits are abundant and in their respective primes. There's nothing like eating a blueberry pie in July. At the bakery we change our flavors with the seasons. In winter, we serve hearty staples like Classic Double-Crust Apple Pie and Maple Bourbon Pecan Pie; in spring and summer, we do Key Lime Meringue and Lattice-Crust Cherry Pie.

Speaking of pies, the highlight of a good pie is the crust. Making a very flaky crust is *muy importante.* Let us say this just once: *There Is No Substitute for Making Your Own Crust.* Even if it looks imperfect.

We bake a lot of specialty cakes for birthdays and weddings, and while they are not the fanciest confections on the planet, they just might be some of the best tasting. We don't like fancy or fussy desserts, and the menu at Clinton St. reflects this. American classics like a Hot Fudge Sundae or Brownies can be transporting when done well. The famed Upper East Side café and ice cream emporium Serendipity was always a great inspiration for us when we first discussed our dessert offerings. As it was located just a few blocks from my grandmother's apartment, I've been a regular there since birth. Serendipity is known for its enormous splurge sundaes and volcanic frozen hot chocolate. The café also features an assortment of fun flavor combinations infused with whimsy and made with care. Now we admire our own sundaes, making sure to punctuate them with Raspberry Caramel Sauce, a cloud of Real Whipped Cream, or some house-made candied nuts. And let's not forget the cherry on top.

CLASSIC WHITE *Birthday Cake*

**MAKES ONE 4-LAYER,
8-INCH CAKE OR EIGHTEEN
3-INCH CUPCAKES**

CAKE

2 CUPS *plus* 1 TABLESPOON *cake
flour*

1½ CUPS *sugar*

1 TABLESPOON *plus* 1 TEASPOON
baking powder

¾ TEASPOON *salt*

1½ STICKS (12 TABLESPOONS)
unsalted butter, softened

1 CUP *whole milk*

1 TABLESPOON *canola oil*

1 TEASPOON *vanilla extract*

4 *large egg whites*

. . . .

OLD-FASHIONED
VANILLA FROSTING

1½ STICKS *unsalted butter, softened*

¼ CUP *vegetable shortening*

3 CUPS *confectioners' sugar*

⅓ CUP *whole milk*

1½ TEASPOONS *vanilla extract*

½ TEASPOON *salt*

1 MAKE THE CAKE: Preheat the oven to 325°F. Lightly grease and flour two 8-inch round cake pans or a standard cupcake pan.

2 Sift all the dry ingredients into a mixing bowl.

3 In the bowl of an electric mixer, beat the butter and ¼ cup of the milk for 2 to 3 minutes, until it is well mixed and holds together. Slowly add the remaining milk and the oil and vanilla. Beat another minute until smooth. Slowly beat in the dry ingredients until well incorporated.

4 In a separate stainless-steel or copper bowl, whip the egg whites until medium peaks form (this will take 4 to 5 minutes by hand, 1 to 2 minutes if you are using an electric mixer with a whip attachment).

5 Fold the whipped whites into the batter (You should not be able to see any whites).

6 Divide the batter between the prepared cake pans or cupcake tins. Bake for 25 to 30 minutes (12 to 14 minutes for cupcakes), until a toothpick inserted into the middle comes out clean.

7 Let the cakes or cupcakes cool and unmold.

8 MAKE THE FROSTING: In a large bowl, cream the butter and shortening until smooth and creamy. Add the sugar, milk, vanilla, and salt and mix until smooth and creamy.

9 ASSEMBLE THE CAKE: Slice each cake in half with a long serrated knife to create 4 thin layers. Place 1 bottom layer, bottom side down, on a cake plate. Ice the top with 3 to 4 tablespoons frosting and repeat with remaining layers, leaving last layer bottom side up (so that the top of cake is flat and even). You will have a 4-layer unfrosted cake. Then use a cake spatula to mask the top and sides until the cake is evenly frosted.

Chocolate Frosting Variation

Follow the vanilla frosting recipe, adding ½ cup unsweetened cocoa powder and ½ cup melted semisweet chocolate.

BLACK & WHITE *Cake*

**MAKES ONE 4-LAYER,
8-INCH CAKE**

CAKE

1½ STICKS (12 TABLESPOONS) *unsalted butter, softened*

1 CUP *light brown sugar*

1 CUP *granulated sugar*

2 *large eggs, plus* **1** *yolk*

1½ CUPS *all-purpose flour*

⅔ CUP *unsweetened cocoa powder, sifted*

2 TEASPOONS *baking powder*

1 TEASPOON *baking soda*

1 CUP *pumpkin puree*

½ CUP *buttermilk*

2 TEASPOONS *vanilla extract*

....

FROSTING

8 OUNCES *cream cheese, softened*

½ STICK (4 TABLESPOONS) *unsalted butter, softened*

4 CUPS *confectioners' sugar*

½ CUP *whole milk*

....

CHOCOLATE GLAZE

½ CUP *heavy cream*

3 TABLESPOONS *light corn syrup*

1 TABLESPOON *unsalted butter*

½ CUP *semisweet chocolate chunks (52–62% cacao; see the Note on page 193)*

Our most popular cake gets its super moistness from a secret ingredient — pumpkin puree.

1 MAKE THE CAKE: Preheat the oven to 300°F. Lightly grease and flour two 8-inch round cake pans.

2 In the bowl of an electric mixer, cream the butter and sugars.

3 Add the eggs and yolk and combine.

4 Whisk the remaining dry ingredients together, in a separate bowl.

5 Whisk the pumpkin puree together with the buttermilk and vanilla in another bowl.

6 Alternate mixing dry ingredients with the pumpkin mixture into the egg mixture. Start with dry and end with wet.

7 Divide the batter between the prepared cake pans. Bake for 30 to 40 minutes, until a toothpick inserted in the middle comes out clean.

8 Let the cakes cool and unmold.

9 MAKE THE FROSTING: In the bowl of an electric mixer, cream the cream cheese and butter together until soft.

10 Add the confectioners' sugar, blending in 1 cup at a time.

11 Add the milk slowly, as needed, and mix until the frosting is smooth and creamy.

12 MAKE THE GLAZE: Heat the heavy cream, corn syrup, and butter in a saucepan until boiling.

13 Place the chocolate in a bowl. Pour the cream mixture over the chocolate until it is completely melted, mixing gently with a rubber spatula until the glaze is smooth.

14 ASSEMBLE THE CAKE: Slice each cake in half with a long serrated knife to create 4 thin layers. Place 1 bottom layer on a cake plate. Ice the top with 3 to 4 tablespoons frosting and repeat with the remaining layers. You will have a 4-layer unfrosted cake. Then use a cake spatula to mask the top and sides until the cake is evenly frosted. Set it in the fridge for 10 minutes. Then remove the cake from the fridge and pour the chocolate glaze over the center of the cake until the top is covered and the glaze runs over the sides, still showing some frosting. Let the glaze set and serve.

COCONUT *Lemon Curd Cake*

MAKES ONE 3-LAYER, 8-INCH CAKE

This cake always reminds us of a giant snowflake, which is why we haul it out during the winter, when people are up for a thick, delicious dessert.

LEMON CURD

½ **CUP** *freshly squeezed lemon juice*

½ **CUP** *plus* **2 TABLESPOONS** *sugar*

1 STICK (8 TABLESPOONS) *unsalted butter*

2 *large eggs*

....

CAKE

2½ **CUPS** *cake flour (measure, then sift)*

1¼ **CUPS** *sugar*

1 TABLESPOON *plus* **1 TEASPOON** *baking powder*

¾ **TEASPOON** *salt*

1½ **STICKS (12 TABLESPOONS)** *unsalted butter, softened*

1 TABLESPOON *canola oil*

1 CUP *whole milk*

1½ **TEASPOONS** *vanilla extract*

5 *large egg whites*

....

FROSTING

8 OUNCES *cream cheese (not whipped)*

½ **STICK (4 TABLESPOONS)** *unsalted butter, softened*

4 CUPS *confectioners' sugar*

½ **CUP** *whole milk*

16 OUNCES *sweetened coconut flakes*

1 MAKE THE LEMON CURD: Boil the lemon juice, sugar, and butter in a medium saucepan.

2 Whisk the eggs together in a large bowl.

3 Pour ½ cup of the lemon mixture into the eggs and whisk together. Add the egg mixture back into the pan with the remaining lemon mixture. Cook on low heat, stirring, until thick, and then strain (use the finest strainer that you can find). Cover and cool in the refrigerator until ready to assemble the cake.

4 MAKE THE CAKE: Preheat the oven to 350°F. Lightly grease and flour an 8-inch round cake pan.

5 Mix together the flour, sugar, baking powder, and salt. Add the butter and oil and mix until small pea-sized balls form. Add the milk and vanilla and mix until smooth.

6 In a separate bowl, whip the egg whites until medium peaks form (this will take 4 to 5 minutes by hand, 1 to 2 minutes if you are using an electric mixer with a whip attachment).

7 Fold the whipped whites into the batter (you should not be able to see any whites, and the batter should look light and fluffy).

8 Pour the batter into the prepared pan and bake for 30 to 35 minutes, until a toothpick inserted in the middle comes out clean.

9 Let the cake cool, then unmold.

10 MAKE THE FROSTING: In the bowl of an electric mixer, cream butter and cream cheese till soft. Add the confectioners' sugar, blending in 1 cup at a time. Add the milk slowly, as needed, and mix until the frosting is smooth and creamy.

11 ASSEMBLE THE CAKE: Slice into 3 layers with a long serrated knife.

12 Reserve the bottom layer. Place another layer on a serving plate. Using a pastry bag, pipe circles of lemon curd on the top using half the curd. Place a second cake layer on top of the first and repeat with the remaining lemon curd. Top with the reserved bottom layer.

13 Refrigerate for 10 minutes to allow the cake to set.

14 Ice the outside of the cake with the frosting.

15 Gently apply coconut to the top and sides of the cake. The frosting will act as a glue to hold the coconut.

FLOURLESS *Chocolate Cake*

MAKES ONE 10-INCH CAKE

1 TABLESPOON *unsalted butter, room temperature*

¼ CUP plus **1 CUP** *sugar*

1¼ CUPS *strong, freshly brewed or cold coffee*

3¾ CUPS *semisweet chocolate chunks (52–62% cacao; see the Note on page 193)*

7 *large eggs*

1¾ CUPS *heavy cream, chilled*

½ CUP *unsweetened cocoa powder, sifted (we recommend Valrhona or Ghirardelli)*

Raspberry Caramel Sauce (page 178)

Real Whipped Cream (optional; page 178)

This cake is rich, dense, and a true chocolate lover's dream. It's also a great flourless dessert for Passover. The secret is the freshly brewed coffee, which makes it really intense, moist, and, well, caffeinated.

1   Preheat the oven to 325°F. Lightly grease a 10-inch springform cake pan. Add ¼ cup of the sugar to the pan. Shake the sugar along the buttered sides and bottom so that the pan is coated. Tap the pan with your fingers to release any excess sugar and discard.

2   If the coffee is hot, pour it over the chocolate chunks in a bowl and whisk quickly to melt the chocolate. If the coffee is not hot, place the chunks and coffee together in a microwave-safe container and heat together for 1 to 2 minutes on high, until the chocolate is melted.

3   Bring a pot of water to a simmer. In a metal or glass bowl, whisk together the eggs with the remaining cup sugar. Place the bowl over the simmering water and whisk continuously until the eggs become light and fluffy.

4   In a separate bowl, whip the cream to medium peaks either by hand or with a handheld mixer.

5   Add the coffee-and-chocolate mixture to the eggs in two stages, folding between each stage. Gently fold in the cocoa powder and then the whipped cream, using the same method.

6   Pour the batter into the prepared pan. Wrap the bottom of the springform in heavy-duty foil. Place the pan in a shallow baking dish and fill the dish with hot tap water until the water comes up 1 to 2 inches along the sides of the pan.

7   Bake for 1 hour and 20 minutes. Turn off the oven, prop open the oven door, and allow the cake to cool in the oven for 30 minutes. Remove the cake from the oven and cool for 2 hours in the fridge or at room temperature.

8   To serve, remove the outer ring of the pan. Cut the cake into clean slices using a knife dipped in warm water and wiped in between slices. Serve with Raspberry Caramel Sauce and Real Whipped Cream.

SALTED *Peanut Butter Sauce*

MAKES 1¼ CUPS

1 CUP *creamy peanut butter*

2 TABLESPOONS *confectioners' sugar*

1 TABLESPOON *salt*

½ TABLESPOON *heavy cream*

3 TABLESPOONS *unsalted butter, melted*

1 Place all the ingredients in a microwave-safe container or bowl. Microwave on high until the peanut butter is hot and the butter has melted. Mix with a whisk until smooth and cool and a sauce has formed.

2 Serve on top of ice cream. Reheat the sauce in the microwave until warm.

ALMOND *Praline Brittle*

MAKES ¾ POUND

2 CUPS *sugar*

1 CUP *light corn syrup*

8 OUNCES *unsalted blanched almonds, coarsely chopped*

1 TEASPOON *baking soda*

1 Cook the sugar and corn syrup together over medium heat in a heavy-bottomed pan until the sugar has dissolved. Pour in the nuts and continue cooking until a piece pulled from the syrup with tongs forms a hard ball when dropped into cold water or until the syrup starts to turn a light amber color. This will take 15 to 20 minutes.

2 Lightly grease a cookie sheet or line the sheet with a Silpat mat.

3 Add the baking soda to the mixture and stir well. Pour the mixture onto the prepared cookie sheet. Do not spread or touch the mixture! It will be extremely hot.

4 When the praline has cooled, break it into pieces. Store it in a tightly covered container at room temperature.

REAL *Whipped Cream*

MAKES 1½ TO 2 CUPS

1 CUP *heavy cream*

⅓ CUP *sugar*

¼ TEASPOON *vanilla extract*

....

NOTE *If you like a sweeter whipped cream, add more sugar to taste.*

When making whipped cream, a medium-sized flexible whisk works best. Let your guests gather in the kitchen while you whip the cream and you are guaranteed a fun time.

In a medium stainless-steel bowl, whisk all the ingredients vigorously until soft peaks form (approximately 3 to 4 minutes). Whisk a few extra times to firm up as desired. Refrigerate until needed.

RASPBERRY *Caramel Sauce*

MAKES 1 CUP

½ CUP *sugar*

3 CUPS *frozen raspberries*

½ TEASPOON *lemon extract or zest*

....

NOTE *This sauce has a great shine to it. It is perfect with chocolate desserts, such as Flourless Chocolate Cake (page 175), or on top of ice cream, bread pudding, or with peach Melba.*

RESTAURANT TRICK *Use a pastry brush, dipped in a small bowl of water, to brush down the sides of the pot while the caramel cooks so that the sugar crystals don't burn onto the pot.*

Neil has been a fan of this sauce for twenty years. He loves it. We often serve it at catering events with our Flourless Chocolate Cake. Even though it's a little bit eighties, people always lick the plate on which it's served.

1 In a heavy-bottomed pot, dissolve the sugar in ¼ cup water with a whisk. Bring the water to boil over medium-high heat and cook until the sugar and water have formed a medium-dark caramel, 8 to 10 minutes. Be careful! The caramel is extremely hot and can burn you.

2 Carefully whisk in the raspberries and lemon extract and cook until the caramel is dissolved and the sauce is liquid, about 5 minutes. Once you add the raspberries, the sugar in the caramel will solidify but should gradually loosen after 1 to 2 minutes. If the caramel sticks to the whisk, run the whisk along the bottom of the pot to melt the caramel.

3 Ladle the sauce into a fine strainer. Press the sauce through the strainer with a heatproof spatula until only the raspberry seeds remain. Cool the sauce.

4 Reheat the amount of sauce you need in the microwave. If the sauce becomes too thick, add hot water to thin it.

HOT FUDGE *Sauce*

MAKES 4 CUPS

½ **CUP** *sugar*

PINCH *of salt*

1 **CUP** *light corn syrup*

½ **CUP** *heavy cream*

½ **STICK (4 TABLESPOONS)** *unsalted butter, cubed*

2 **TEASPOONS** *vanilla extract*

2½ **CUPS** *semisweet chocolate chunks (52–62% cacao; see the Note on page 193)*

1¾ **CUPS** *unsweetened cocoa powder, sifted*

1   Mix the sugar and the salt. In a heavy-bottomed saucepan over medium heat, warm the sugar mixture, corn syrup, cream, and ½ cup water together until the sugar is dissolved; there is no need to stir.

2   Increase the heat to medium-high and simmer 4 minutes while stirring. Remove the pot from the heat and whisk in the butter and vanilla until the butter melts and the sauce begins to come together.

3   Return the pot to the heat and whisk in the chocolate chunks. Once the chocolate is melted, whisk in half of the cocoa powder until combined and then whisk in the remaining amount. Pull the pot off the heat and continue to whisk the sides and the middle of the pot. The sauce will become thick and black as well as shiny. Return the sauce to the heat for 30 seconds to ensure that no lumps remain.

4   Transfer the sauce to a container, cool, and place in the fridge (although this sauce may never get that far!). It will keep for 6 to 8 weeks, refrigerated.

5   Reheat only what you need in the microwave. Add milk or cream to thin the sauce, if needed.

BANANAS *Foster*

SERVES 2

1 **TABLESPOON** *unsalted butter*

⅓ **CUP** *light brown sugar*

3 *medium-ripe bananas, cut on the bias into 1-inch slices*

2 **TABLESPOONS** *cinnamon sugar (2 tablespoons sugar and ¼ tablespoon cinnamon)*

½ **TEASPOON** *vanilla extract*

3 **TABLESPOONS** *dark rum*

Vanilla ice cream

Easy to make and ridiculously delicious, this is a quick dessert you can whip up and still use to impress. Or serve it over pancakes for a decadent brunch dish. Stop your prep after step 1 and you've got the perfect topping for your morning oatmeal. Just add toasted almonds or pecans and you're in business.

1   In a 9-inch sauté pan over high heat, lightly brown the butter. Once it is past the foaming stage, add the sugar and cook until melted. Use a spoon to break up any sugar lumps. Add the bananas and mix until coated. Sprinkle the cinnamon sugar over the bananas. Cook until the bananas become golden brown, but not mushy and overcooked. Be careful to keep the pan steady so that the bananas will caramelize.

2   Remove the pan from the stove and add the vanilla extract and dark rum. Carefully light a match over the pan and allow the mixture to flambé. Cook for 30 seconds and remove from the heat. Serve warm over vanilla ice cream.

PUMPKIN *Cheesecake*

GRAHAM CRACKER CRUST

2 CUPS *graham-cracker crumbs*

¼ CUP *sugar*

½ TEASPOON *vanilla extract*

1 STICK (8 TABLESPOONS) *unsalted butter, melted*

....

CHEESECAKE BATTER

1½ CUPS *(three 8-ounce packages) cream cheese, room temperature*

1 CUP *sour cream, room temperature*

1 CUP *sugar*

1 TABLESPOON *vanilla extract*

1½ TEASPOONS *cinnamon*

¼ TEASPOON *nutmeg*

¼ TEASPOON *allspice*

PINCH *of ground ginger*

PINCH *of ground cloves*

1 CUP *pumpkin puree, room temperature*

2 TABLESPOONS *heavy cream*

3 *large eggs*

....

NOTE *To make a water bath, use any roasting pan that is large enough to hold the pan in which you are baking. Try a roasting pan with two handles. It's a good idea to wrap your springform pan in heavy-duty foil before adding water to the roasting pan. Use hot tap water for the bath and make sure the water level is at least 1 inch up the sides of the pan but not so high that water will splash into the springform.*

This cheesecake is my favorite Thanksgiving treat. It's elegant yet rich, and the pumpkin flavor and color is very subtle. This cake is on the smaller side, but you need only a thin sliver to enjoy.

1 Preheat the oven to 350°F. Coat a 10-inch springform pan with nonstick cooking spray.

2 MAKE THE CRUST: Mix the graham-cracker crumbs, sugar, and vanilla in a small bowl. Stir in the melted butter until all the ingredients are well mixed.

3 Turn the crust mixture into the prepared pan and spread evenly over the bottom (but *not* up the sides). Press down firmly to form a crust.

4 Bake for 15 minutes. Remove the crust from the oven and, let cool, while you start on the cheesecake batter. Turn down the oven temperature to 325°F.

5 MAKE THE BATTER: In the bowl of an electric mixer, blend the cream cheese, sour cream, sugar, vanilla, and spices until smooth. Add the pumpkin puree and heavy cream and mix until combined.

6 Add the eggs one at a time, until the mixture is smooth. Do not overmix.

7 ASSEMBLE THE CHEESECAKE: Pour the batter over the baked crust.

8 Bake for 1 hour in a water bath (see Note).

9 Turn off the oven, prop open the oven door, and allow the cake to cool for 10 minutes. Remove the cake from oven and cool completely in the fridge overnight.

10 Cut with a hot knife and serve.

CLASSIC DOUBLE-CRUST *Apple Pie*

DOUGH

2¼ CUPS *all-purpose flour, plus*
¼ CUP *for rolling out the dough*

1¼ STICKS (10 TABLESPOONS) *cold unsalted butter, cut into small cubes*

3 TABLESPOONS *cold or room-temperature vegetable shortening*

3 TABLESPOONS *sugar*

PINCH *of salt*

½ CUP *plus* **2 TABLESPOONS** *cold whole milk*

....

FILLING

8 *medium to large local farm apples*

½ CUP *granulated sugar*

¼ CUP *dark brown sugar*

2 TABLESPOONS *all-purpose flour*

Zest of 1 small lemon

1 TABLESPOON *freshly squeezed lemon juice*

1 TEASPOON *vanilla extract*

1½ TEASPOONS *cinnamon*

1 PINCH *of nutmeg*

....

2 TABLESPOONS *heavy cream, for brushing on top of the dough*

2 TO 3 TABLESPOONS *granulated sugar, for sprinkling on top of the pie*

Make this pie with a mix of tart and sweet, hard and medium-hard, apples. Or any mixture of these varieties: Mutsu, Granny Smith, Cortland, Jonagold, Empire.

1 MAKE THE DOUGH: With your hands, 2 forks, or a pastry blender, combine all ingredients except the milk into a mixing bowl, until the butter and shortening form pea-sized pieces. Add the milk and mix until incorporated and a dough forms. Do not overmix. Divide the dough in half and wrap each half in plastic wrap. Let rest for an hour in the refrigerator.

2 MAKE THE FILLING: Trim tops and bottoms of the apples. Peel, core, and slice the apples into eighths (or cut with an apple wedger) and put into a bowl. Add the remaining filling ingredients and combine until the apples are well coated.

3 ASSEMBLE THE PIE: Preheat the oven to 350°F. Roll out half the dough on a lightly floured surface to form a circle that is 10 inches in diameter, ¼ inch thick. Line a 9-inch deep-dish pie pan with the rolled-out dough. Brush the rim of the dough with water or milk.

4 Mound the filling into the pie shell.

5 Roll out the other half of the dough, place over the filling, and seal the edges. Crimp the edges of the crust.

6 Brush the top crust with the heavy cream and sprinkle with additional sugar. Cut a 1-inch airhole in the center of pie.

7 Bake for 1 hour to 75 minutes, until the crust is dark golden brown and the apples are tender to the knife.

8 Cool the pie and serve plain or with vanilla ice cream.

LATTICE-CRUST CHERRY *Pie*

MAKES ONE 9-INCH PIE

DOUGH

2¼ CUPS *all-purpose flour, plus*
¼ CUP *for rolling out the dough*

1¼ STICKS (10 TABLESPOONS) *cold unsalted butter, cut into small cubes*

3 TABLESPOONS *cold or room-temperature vegetable shortening*

3 TABLESPOONS *sugar*

PINCH *of salt*

½ CUP *plus* **2 TABLESPOONS** *cold whole milk*

....

FILLING

6 CUPS *pitted sour cherries (fresh or frozen)*

¾ CUP *sugar*

3 TABLESPOONS *cornstarch*

1 TABLESPOON *freshly squeezed lemon juice*

1 TEASPOON *vanilla extract*

¼ TEASPOON *cinnamon*

....

2 TABLESPOONS *heavy cream, for brushing on top of the dough*

2 TO 4 TABLESPOONS *sugar, for sprinkling on top of the pie*

Sour cherries are best for this pie, but if they're out of season or you can't get them, you can substitute sweet cherries.

1   MAKE THE DOUGH: With your hands, 2 forks, or a pastry blender, combine all ingredients except the milk into a mixing bowl, until the butter and shortening form pea-sized pieces. Add the milk and mix until incorporated and a dough forms. Do not overmix. Divide the dough in half and wrap each half in plastic wrap. Let rest for an hour in the refrigerator.

2   MAKE THE FILLING: Mix all the ingredients together in a bowl with your hands. Set aside.

3   ASSEMBLE THE PIE: Preheat the oven to 350°F. Roll out half the dough on a lightly floured surface to form a circle that is 10 inches in diameter, ¼ inch thick. Line a 9-inch pie pan with the rolled-out dough. Scrape the filling into the pie shell. Refrigerate while you roll out the rest of the dough to the same diameter and thickness as the first half.

4   Use a knife or pastry wheel to slice ¾-inch strips horizontally across the dough.

5   Brush the bottom edge of the pie shell with a little water so that it becomes sticky but not waterlogged. Divide the lattice strips into 2 equal groups. To make the lattice into a crisscross pattern, lay the first group of strips across the pie ½ to ¾ inch apart, making sure to press both ends onto the pie shell edge. Use the remaining strips to make the vertical crossings by weaving 1 strip at a time over the first strip and under the second strip. Repeat the process until the strip has reached the end of the pie. Gently press the strip onto the edge. Place the second strip ½ to ¾ inch from the first strip and repeat until all of the vertical strips are in place and a lattice pattern has been created. Trim any excess dough from the edge.

6   Brush the lattice with heavy cream and sprinkle with additional sugar. Place the pie plate on a cookie sheet to prevent any juices from leaking into your oven. Bake for 50 minutes, until the lattice is golden brown.

MAPLE BOURBON PECAN *Pie*

MAKES ONE 9-INCH PIE

DOUGH

2¼ CUPS *all-purpose flour, plus*
¼ CUP *for rolling out the dough*

1¼ STICKS (10 TABLESPOONS) *cold unsalted butter, cut into small cubes*

3 TABLESPOONS *cold or room-temperature vegetable shortening*

3 TABLESPOONS *sugar*

PINCH *of salt*

½ CUP *plus* **2 TABLESPOONS** *cold whole milk*

....

FILLING

2 CUPS *pecan pieces*

1 CUP *dark corn syrup*

½ CUP *maple syrup*

½ CUP *sugar*

3 *large eggs*

½ STICK (4 TABLESPOONS) *unsalted butter, melted*

4 TABLESPOONS *Maker's Mark or Jack Daniel's bourbon*

1 TEASPOON *vanilla extract*

This is our signature Thanksgiving pie — the perfect closure to your holiday feast. It's surprisingly *not* gooey-sweet and has an addictive chewy texture when cooled and rested. At our table, we serve it warm, with vanilla ice cream, but I like it best late at night, slightly chilled.

The dough recipe makes enough for two pies. Double the filling recipe or freeze half the dough for another time.

1 MAKE THE PASTRY DOUGH: With your hands, 2 forks, or a pastry blender, combine all ingredients except the milk into a mixing bowl, until the butter and shortening form pea-sized pieces. Add the milk and mix until incorporated and a dough forms. Do not overmix. Divide the dough in half and wrap each half in plastic wrap. Let half the dough rest for an hour in the refrigerator. Freeze the other half or chill it in the refrigerator if you plan to bake a second pie in just a few days.

2 MAKE THE FILLING: In a large bowl, whisk all the ingredients together until well combined. Set aside.

3 ASSEMBLE THE PIE: Preheat the oven to 325°F. Roll out the chilled dough on a lightly floured surface to form a circle that is 10 inches in diameter, ¼ inch thick. Line a 9-inch pie pan with the rolled-out dough. Crimp the edges of the crust.

4 Pour the filling into the pie shell.

5 Bake at 325°F for 30 minutes, then turn down the oven to 300°F. Bake for another 25 minutes, until pie is set.

6 Cool and serve.

KEY LIME MERINGUE *Pie*

MAKES ONE 9-INCH PIE

GRAHAM CRACKER CRUST

¾ CUP *graham-cracker crumbs*

½ STICK (4 TABLESPOONS) *unsalted butter, melted*

2 TABLESPOONS *sugar*

¼ TEASPOON *vanilla extract*

....

FILLING

¾ CUP *Key lime juice*

ONE 14-OUNCE CAN *sweetened condensed milk*

4 *large egg yolks*

Zest of 1 green lime

....

MERINGUE

2 *large egg whites*

1 CUP *sugar*

....

NOTE *Don't worry if the meringue texture is initially gritty. Once the meringue bakes in the oven, the sugar will dissolve and caramelize.*

TRY THIS *Use a measuring cup or the edge of a soup can to press the Graham Cracker Crust against the sides of the pie plate in order to make an even crust with thick sides.*

Our son, Alex, has never met a Key lime pie he didn't like. But he especially loves ours. The key (pun intended) is to use real Key limes, but if you must, fresh Key lime juice is available in some specialty stores. And if all else fails, you can use regular limes. At Clinton St. we top our pie with a sweet fresh meringue that is crackly and crunchy on the outside and creamy underneath. It is the perfect complement to the tart lime filling. For those who don't love meringue, or don't have time to make it, our Real Whipped Cream (page 178) and some freshly grated lime zest work beautifully.

1 Preheat the oven to 350°F.

2 MAKE THE CRUST: Mix the graham-cracker crumbs and melted butter in a small bowl. Add the sugar and vanilla.

3 Press the mixture evenly onto the bottom and sides of a pie pan. Bake for 10 minutes. Then turn down the oven temperature to 325°F. Remove the crust from the oven and let cool.

4 MAKE THE FILLING: While the crust is baking, whisk together the filling ingredients. Fill the prebaked crust with the filling and bake at 325°F for 8 to 10 minutes, until the filling is set. The filling may still jiggle in the center but should have the texture of a firm pudding or custard. Remove the pie from the oven and return the oven temperature to 350°F.

5 MAKE THE MERINGUE: Warm the egg whites in the microwave for 10 to 15 seconds on high (in a microwave-safe bowl or container) until they are warm to the touch. Place the whites in a clean bowl and use a standing mixer or a handheld mixer on medium speed to whisk together the warmed egg whites. Gradually add the sugar and turn up the speed to high. The goal is to get the meringue to soft peaks with a marshmallowy consistency. You will have to mix for 3 to 4 minutes to get the meringue to this stage.

6 Use a spatula to gently swirl the meringue on top of the pie without pressing down too hard. Use the spatula to make peaks and craters so that the meringue topping looks rustic and natural. Bake at 350°F for 10 to 12 minutes, until the meringue is golden and crusty.

7 Chill the pie overnight in the refrigerator.

CLASSIC DOUBLE-CRUST PEACH *Pie*

MAKES ONE 9-INCH PIE

DOUGH

2¼ **CUPS** *all-purpose flour, plus*
¼ **CUP** *for rolling out the dough*

1¼ **STICKS (10 TABLESPOONS)** *cold unsalted butter, cut into small cubes*

3 **TABLESPOONS** *cold or room-temperature vegetable shortening*

3 **TABLESPOONS** *sugar*

PINCH *of salt*

½ **CUP** *plus* 2 **TABLESPOONS** *cold whole milk*

....

FILLING

8 *medium to large fresh peaches (we recommend yellow freestone peaches)* or 8 **CUPS** *frozen sliced peaches, thawed*

½ **CUP** *granulated sugar*

¼ **CUP** *dark brown sugar*

2 **TABLESPOONS** *all-purpose flour*

Zest of 1 small lemon

1 **TABLESPOON** *freshly squeezed lemon juice*

1 **TEASPOON** *vanilla*

1½ *teaspoons cinnamon*

1 *pinch of nutmeg*

....

2 **TABLESPOONS** *heavy cream, for brushing on top of the dough*

2 **TO** 3 **TABLESPOONS** *granulated sugar, for sprinkling on top of pie*

....

NOTE *To peel fresh peaches, blanch whole peaches in a pot of boiling water for 10 seconds. Plunge the peaches into a bowl of ice water. The skins will peel off easily.*

Nothing says summer better than peach pie. Peaches cook well, require minimal prep, and reap big rewards when baked in a crust and served with a scoop of cold vanilla ice cream. Yum!

1 MAKE THE DOUGH: With your hands, 2 forks, or a pastry blender, combine all the ingredients except the milk into a mixing bowl, until the butter and shortening form pea-sized pieces. Add the milk and mix until incorporated and a dough forms. Do not overmix. Divide the dough in half and wrap each half in plastic wrap. Let rest for an hour in the refrigerator.

2 MAKE THE FILLING: If using fresh peaches, peel and halve them, remove the pits, and slice each one into eighths. Add remaining filling ingredients and combine until the peaches are well coated.

3 ASSEMBLE THE PIE: Preheat the oven to 350°F. Roll out half the dough on a lightly floured surface to form a circle that is 10 inches in diameter, ¼ inch thick. Line a 9-inch pie pan with the rolled-out dough. Scrape the filling into the pie shell. Refrigerate while you roll out the rest of the dough to the same diameter and thickness as the first half.

4 Use a knife or pastry wheel to slice ¾-inch strips horizontally across the dough.

5 Brush the bottom edge of the pie shell with a little water so that it becomes sticky but not waterlogged. Divide the lattice strips into 2 equal groups. To make the lattice into a crisscross pattern, lay the first group of strips across the pie ½ to ¾ inch apart, making sure to press both ends onto the pie shell edge. Use the remaining strips to make the vertical crossings by weaving 1 strip at a time over the first strip and under the second strip. Repeat the process until the strip has reached the end of the pie. Gently press the strip onto the edge. Place the second strip ½ to ¾ inch from the first strip and repeat until all of the vertical strips are in place and a lattice pattern has been created. Trim any excess dough from the edge.

6 Brush the lattice with heavy cream and sprinkle with additional sugar. Place the pie plate on a cookie sheet to prevent any juices from leaking into your oven. Bake for 50 minutes, until the lattice is golden brown.

BROOKIES

MAKES 18 TO 20

1 TABLESPOON *canola oil*

1 TEASPOON *unsalted butter*

2 CUPS *semisweet chocolate chunks (52–62% cacao)*

2 *large eggs*

¾ CUP *light brown sugar*

½ TEASPOON *vanilla extract*

½ CUP *all-purpose flour*

¼ TEASPOON *baking powder*

¼ TEASPOON *salt*

....

NOTE *At the bakery we use a semisweet and a bittersweet chocolate made by Callebaut. We also recommend Scharffen Berger, Ghirardelli, or Valrhona.*

The best way to cut chunks from a bar of chocolate is to use a heavy chef's knife and chop the chocolate as if you were chopping an onion. Cut it one way in strips, and then across, the other way, to make chunks. This method is good for chocolate chunks that will be folded into a batter, like this one, or for a recipe in which you want to bite a piece of chocolate (like a chocolate chunk cookie). For recipes that call for melted chocolate, the smaller you cut the chocolate, the faster it will melt in a double boiler. Bittersweet chocolate and new gourmet chocolates that list their percentages of cacao are best for eating and baking recipes. They have less sugar and more pronounced flavors that are best for recipes like a flourless chocolate cake or a chocolate sauce.

A Brookie is a cross between a brownie and a cookie. The Brookie was originally developed by Ernie Rich, a former colleague of Neil's and now a seasoned pastry chef in his own right. When we first started up the bakery and were looking for a full-time pastry chef, Ernie moonlighted for us. This Brookie is his baby. Good luck eating just one!

1   Preheat the oven to 350°F. If using a convection oven, set it to 325°F.

2   Melt the oil, butter, and 1 cup of the chocolate together in a microwave-safe bowl in the microwave on high heat. Stir the mixture at 1-minute intervals. The total time to melt this mixture will be 2½ to 3 minutes. Or melt the mixture in the stainless-steel bowl of a double boiler. Let cool.

3   In another bowl, with a whisk, mix the eggs, brown sugar, and vanilla together until combined.

4   Fold the melted chocolate mixture into the egg mixture.

5   In another bowl, whisk together the remaining dry ingredients. Add the flour mixture into the chocolate mixture, mix until combined, and then fold in the remaining chocolate chunks.

6   Freeze the batter in a shallow pan (such as a pie plate) for 6 to 8 minutes until the batter sets and hardens slightly.

7   Coat 2 cookie sheets with nonstick cooking spray or line with parchment paper. Scoop about 10 tablespoon-sized Brookies onto each sheet. Bake for 11 to 12 minutes (or 8 to 10 minutes in a convection oven), until the tops look dry and cracked (the insides will still be quite moist). Cool completely. The Brookies will be perfectly soft and chewy.

Variation

For alternate flavor combinations, try white chocolate chunks, walnuts, or peanut butter chunks in place of the semisweet chocolate chunks.

BROWNIES

MAKES 12 BROWNIES

2⅓ **CUPS** *semisweet chocolate chunks (52–62% cacao)*

2 **CUPS** *sugar*

2 **STICKS (16 TABLESPOONS)** *unsalted butter, cubed*

5 *large eggs*

½ **TEASPOON** *vanilla extract*

2 **CUPS** *all-purpose flour (minus 1½ tablespoons)*

½ **TEASPOON** *baking powder*

½ **TEASPOON** *salt*

....

RESTAURANT TRICK *To fold properly, spin the bowl clockwise while using a rubber spatula to fold in the ingredients counterclockwise.*

COMMON MISTAKE *Don't overmix the batter, or the brownies will end up tough, instead of chewy and moist. It is also important to cool the brownies after baking so that they can be cut easily.*

These brownies are rich, dense, and very chocolaty, with an almost fudgy consistency. The better the quality of chocolate you use, the better the brownie. And of course adding chocolate chunks guarantees something quite special. For dinner at the bakery, we serve this "all the way," with vanilla ice cream, Hot Fudge Sauce, Real Whipped Cream, triple chocolate sprinkles, and a real Burgundy or sour cherry.

1   Preheat the oven to 350°F. If using a convection oven, set it to 325°F. Lightly grease a 9-by-12-inch pan, then line the pan with parchment paper to prevent sticking, and grease the paper.

2   Melt the chocolate, sugar, and butter together in a microwave-safe bowl in the microwave on high heat. Stir at 1-minute intervals. The total time to melt this mixture will be 2½ to 3 minutes. Or melt the mixture in the stainless-steel bowl of a double boiler. Let cool.

3   Whisk the eggs and vanilla extract into the warm chocolate mixture.

4   Sift the dry ingredients into a separate bowl.

5   In two stages, gently fold the dry ingredients into the wet batter until combined.

6   Evenly distribute the batter into the prepared pan. Top with a flavoring ingredient, if desired (see Variations).

7   Bake the brownies for 25 minutes, until the top is cracked and the center is still fudgy.

8   Allow the brownies to cool in the refrigerator overnight and cut into approximately 3-inch squares once cooled.

9   Remove the brownies from the pan and trim the edges.

Variations

PEANUT BUTTER *Dollop ½ cup softened peanut butter (not natural) over the batter before baking the brownies. Use the tip of a butter knife to go back and forth through the peanut butter and brownie batter, vertically and horizontally, to make a feathered design.*

NUTS *Add ½ cup sliced almonds or chopped walnuts to the batter.*

CHOCOLATE CHUNK *Add ½ cup semisweet chocolate chunks (see the Note on page 193) to the batter.*

PEPPERMINT *Add 1 teaspoon peppermint extract to the batter.*

PEPPERMINT GLAZE *In a small bowl, whisk 2 tablespoons plus 2 teaspoons milk and ¼ teaspoon peppermint extract. Add 1¼ cups confectioners' sugar and whisk until smooth. Drizzle over the baked and cooled brownies.*

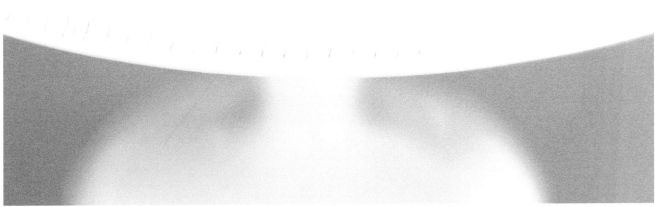

CHOCOLATE CHUNK *Cookies*

MAKES 12 TO 14 COOKIES

1½ STICKS (12 TABLESPOONS) *unsalted butter, room temperature*

¾ CUP *light brown sugar*

½ CUP *granulated sugar*

¼ TEASPOON *vanilla extract*

¼ TEASPOON *cinnamon*

2 *large eggs*

1½ CUPS *all-purpose flour*

1½ TEASPOONS *baking soda*

½ TEASPOON *salt*

1½ CUPS *semisweet chocolate chunks (see the Note on page 193)*

....

NOTE *Do not flatten the scoops of cookie dough. Allow them to keep their round shape and they will flatten naturally in the oven.*

1   Preheat the oven to 350°F. If using a convection oven, turn the oven to 325°F.

2   In the bowl of an electric mixer, cream together the butter, sugars, vanilla, and cinnamon on medium speed, making sure to stop and scrape the bowl down. This will take 3 to 4 minutes.

3   Add the eggs and mix on medium-low speed until combined.

4   Whisk together the flour, baking soda, and salt in a separate bowl and add all at once to the batter. Mix the dough together on low speed until combined, making sure to stop and scrape down the bowl so that all the flour is incorporated.

5   Fold the chocolate chunks into the dough with a spatula or spoon.

6   Flatten the dough into a shallow pan (such as a pie plate) and freeze for 20 minutes.

7   Coat 2 cookie sheets with nonstick cooking spray or line them with parchment paper (we do both at the bakery to prevent sticking). With a 2-ounce ice cream scooper, scoop cookies onto each sheet. You should have 12 to 14 cookies. Bake for 15 to 17 minutes, until golden and just set on top. Let cool.

PEANUT BUTTER *Cookies*

MAKES 12 COOKIES

1 STICK (8 TABLESPOONS) *unsalted butter, room temperature*

½ CUP *peanut butter (chunky or smooth, not natural)*

½ CUP *light brown sugar*

½ CUP *granulated sugar, plus more for sprinkling*

1 *large egg*

1 ¼ CUPS *all-purpose flour*

½ TEASPOON *baking powder*

¼ TEASPOON *baking soda*

¼ TEASPOON *salt*

This recipe can be made with smooth peanut butter or, for a little more texture, chunky. It is so easy and quick that you can whip up a batch for last-minute guests — particularly those four feet and under.

1 Preheat the oven to 325°F.

2 In the bowl of an electric mixer, cream the butter, peanut butter, and sugars together until fluffy.

3 Add the egg and the dry ingredients and mix until smooth.

4 Roll the dough into a log (2 inches thick and 8 inches long) and use a knife to make ¾-inch-thick slices.

5 Coat 2 cookie sheets with nonstick cooking spray or line them with parchment paper (we do both at the bakery to prevent sticking). Place the cookie slices on the sheets.

6 Using the back of a fork, flatten the cookies and make the classic crosshatch design (press hard!). Then sprinkle lightly with granulated sugar.

7 Bake for 15 to 18 minutes, or until light brown. Cool and serve.

Variation

For peanut butter chocolate chunk cookies, add ½ cup semisweet chocolate chunks (see the Note on page 193) after the dry ingredients. You can use a spoon or scoop to portion these cookies rather than rolling the dough into a log.

MAPLE WALNUT *Cookies*

MAKES 24 COOKIES

1 STICK (8 TABLESPOONS) *unsalted butter, room temperature*

½ CUP *sugar, plus more for sprinkling*

¼ CUP *maple syrup*

1 *large egg yolk*

¾ TEASPOON *vanilla extract*

1 ¾ CUPS *all-purpose flour*

1 CUP *walnuts (or pecans), toasted*

These cookies are made from dough that you can roll, slice, and bake like a shortbread. Not too sweet, they're great confections for dunking in coffee.

1 Preheat the oven to 350°F.

2 In the bowl of an electric mixer, cream together the butter and sugar for 3 to 4 minutes, until combined. Scrape down the sides of the bowl. Add the maple syrup, yolk, and vanilla and mix until smooth and combined, again scraping down the sides of the bowl.

3 Add the flour and turn the speed to low. Mix until combined and a dough forms. Add the nuts and briefly mix until they are evenly dispersed in the dough.

4 Roll the dough into a log (2 inches thick and 12 inches long) and wrap it in plastic. Chill in the fridge for 30 minutes, until firm.

5 Coat 2 cookie sheets with nonstick cooking spray or line them with parchment paper (we do both at the bakery to prevent sticking).

6 Remove the dough from the fridge, unwrap, and use a knife to make ½-inch-thick slices. Then sprinkle lightly with sugar.

7 Place 12 cookies on each cookie sheet. Bake for 15 minutes, or until pale golden brown. The cookies should have a brown colored ring around the exterior and the undersides will be a golden brown.

HOT FUDGE *Sundae*

SERVES 1

5 TABLESPOONS *Hot Fudge Sauce (page 179)*

3 LARGE SCOOPS *of vanilla ice cream (preferably artisanal)*

Real Whipped Cream (page 178)

Chocolate sprinkles

1 TO 2 *sweet cherries*

If you are a hot fudge fan (i.e., fanatic), then you know drippy, runny chocolate syrup is no stand-in for the real thing. Hot fudge should be thick, rich, and able to harden against a cold scoop or two, creating a gooey, clingy mass. The best hot fudge I ever ate was from the original Grunnings, a popular restaurant and ice cream chain in New Jersey, near Maplewood, where my Grandpa Tiger lived. A Grunnings run during our holiday visits was de rigueur, and everyone looked forward to one of those killer hot fudge sundaes with very fine ice cream. Neil's own hot fudge is identical to my memory of the one from Grunnings: It's so decadent that real chocoholics (like my mother, for instance) have been known to order a sundae at Clinton St. at 10:00 a.m. She figures, Why save the best for last?

1 If necessary, briefly reheat the Hot Fudge Sauce in the microwave or on the stove. If the sauce is too thick, add more cream or milk to thin it out to the desired consistency.

2 Fill the bottom of a sundae glass with 3 tablespoons of the Hot Fudge Sauce. Top with 1 large scoop of ice cream. Layer with 1 tablespoon of Hot Fudge Sauce and another large scoop of ice cream. Repeat the process once more.

3 Top with a large spoonful of Real Whipped Cream and chocolate sprinkles. Finish with 1 or 2 cherries.

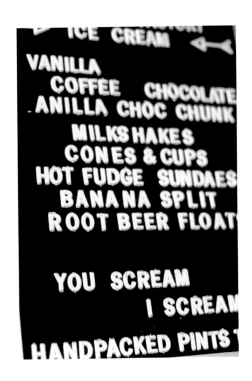

CLASSIC EXTRA-THICK *Shake*

SERVES 1

2 GENEROUS SCOOPS *local, artisanal soft vanilla ice cream (we prefer Brooklyn Ice Cream Factory)*

½ CUP *whole milk*

Real Whipped Cream (page 178)

Chocolate sprinkles

....

NOTE *Each scoop should be a little smaller than a baseball. There will be some leftover milk shake in the blender at the end to enjoy.*

For an even thicker shake, add less milk or more ice cream.

1   Blend the ice cream and milk together in a blender for 1 to 2 minutes, until no chunks remain.

2   Serve in a sundae glass (don't forget the straw!) topped with Real Whipped Cream and chocolate sprinkles.

Variations

Add warm Salted Peanut Butter Sauce (page 176) or half a ripe banana, thinly sliced. Or add warm Salted Peanut Butter Sauce and substitute chocolate ice cream for vanilla.

BLACK & WHITE *Milk Shake*

SERVES 1

2 GENEROUS SCOOPS *local, artisanal soft vanilla ice cream (we prefer Brooklyn Ice Cream Factory)*

⅓ CUP *whole milk*

3 TABLESPOONS *chocolate syrup (we prefer Fox's U-Bet)*

Real Whipped Cream (page 178)

Chocolate sprinkles

1   Blend the ice cream, milk, and chocolate syrup together in a blender for 1 to 2 minutes, until no chunks remain.

2   Serve in a sundae glass (don't forget the straw!) topped with Real Whipped Cream and chocolate sprinkles.

TOFFEE-COFFEE *Milk Shake*

SERVES 1

2 GENEROUS SCOOPS *local, artisanal soft coffee ice cream (we prefer Brooklyn Ice Cream Factory)*

3 TABLESPOONS *Kahlúa*

2 TABLESPOONS *whole milk*

¼ CUP *freshly brewed espresso, room temperature*

Real Whipped Cream (page 178)

Chocolate sprinkles

....

NOTE *You can make a virgin milk shake by substituting 3 tablespoons whole milk for the Kahlúa.*

1   Blend the ice cream, Kahlúa, milk, and espresso together in a blender for 1 to 2 minutes, until no chunks remain.

2   Serve in a sundae glass (don't forget the straw!) topped with Real Whipped Cream and chocolate sprinkles.

ITHACA *Root Beer Float*

SERVES 1

3 GENEROUS SCOOPS *local, artisanal soft vanilla ice cream (we prefer Brooklyn Ice Cream Factory)*

ONE 12-OUNCE BOTTLE *Ithaca Root Beer (or brand of your choice)*

Neil is a sucker for an old-fashioned root beer float, and when he tasted Ithaca root beer for the first time, he knew it was worthy of the greatest float ever poured. Made by a family near the Finger Lakes of New York, Ithaca root beer is nutty, creamy, not too sweet, and has the subtle essence of star anise, juniper berries, and vanilla bean. Best of all, it retains its carbonation. We think it's the best root beer around, hands down, but of course any root beer of your choice will do.

1 Place 2 scoops ice cream in a tall glass. Pour in about 3 ounces root beer. As the foam settles, pour in the remaining root beer.

2 Garnish in the old-fashioned style, with the remaining scoop of ice cream on the side of the glass, like a lemon wedge.

10

. DRINKS .

Our drinks menu evolved to complement our food. You can't, after all, serve brunch dishes without a Bloody Mary or a Mimosa! Whether it's Lime Squash in summer or Hot Buttered Cider in winter, we let the menu dictate what to offer. Here are our most delicious recipes.

HOT *Chocolate*

SERVES 4

9 TABLESPOONS *sugar*

3 TABLESPOONS *unsweetened cocoa powder (we recommend Valrhona or Ghirardelli)*

3 CUPS *warm or steamed milk*

Real Whipped Cream (page 178)

1   Whisk together the sugar and cocoa powder. Add 3 tablespoons of the mixture to each of 4 mugs. Add 1 teaspoon hot water to each mug and stir to dissolve the powder. Add ¾ cup warm or steamed milk to each mug. Stir to combine.

2   Top with Real Whipped Cream.

HOT BUTTERED *Cider*

SERVES 4

1 QUART *freshly pressed apple cider*

½ CUP *dark rum*

½ CUP *warm Maple Butter (page 78)*

4 *cinnamon sticks*

DASH *of freshly grated nutmeg, for sprinkling*

1   In a medium saucepan, whisk together the apple cider, rum, and Maple Butter until combined. Add the cinnamon sticks and warm over medium heat.

2   Pour into 4 mugs (with 1 cinnamon stick each) and garnish with a sprinkle of freshly grated nutmeg.

APPLE *Bourbon Cobblers*

SERVES 4

8 OUNCES *bourbon*

20 OUNCES *freshly pressed apple cider*

2 CUPS *Boylan's ginger ale (or brand of your choice)*

4 *cinnamon sticks*

Fill 4 tumbler glasses with ice. Pour 2 ounces bourbon and 5 ounces apple cider into each glass. Top each glass with approximately ½ cup ginger ale and serve with a cinnamon stick.

LIME SQUASH

SERVES 4

¼ CUP *fresh lime juice*

¼ CUP *Simple Syrup (recipe follows)*

Ice

Seltzer water

Lime wedge

We discovered this drink in Antigua while vacationing at Harmony Hall, known for its remote location and critically acclaimed restaurant perched high above the sparkling Caribbean. Every afternoon, Neil and I would relax on the stone patio and sip a fresh Lime Squash, delivered to the table in a tall frosted glass with a lavender napkin tied around its middle. Neither of us had ever tasted a more refreshing beverage. At brunch we serve this drink spiked with vodka.

Pour the lime juice and Simple Syrup into 4 tall glasses. Add ice to fill three-quarters of each glass. Pour seltzer over the ice to fill and stir. Add a lime wedge to each rim. Serve immediately.

Simple Syrup

1 CUP *sugar*

Bring 2 cups water to a boil in a saucepan. Stir the sugar into the boiling water. Once the sugar is dissolved completely, remove the pan from the heat. Allow to cool and refrigerate in a closed jar. The syrup will keep for many months.

SPICY BLOODY MARYS

ONE 46-OUNCE CAN *Sacramento Tomato Juice (or brand of your choice)*

¼ CUP *plus* **2 TABLESPOONS** *prepared or freshly grated horseradish*

3 TABLESPOONS *freshly squeezed lemon juice*

1½ TABLESPOONS *salt*

1 TABLESPOON *plus* **1 TEASPOON** *ground black pepper*

1 TABLESPOON *Tabasco sauce*

1 TABLESPOON *Worcestershire sauce*

1 TEASPOON *ground celery seed*

18 OUNCES *vodka*

12 STALKS *celery*

12 SLICES *lemon*

We like a Bloody Mary that opens up the appetite, has some good character and the right seasonings, and is addictive enough to make you want seconds. Horseradish is a must. We can't think of a more perfect match than Bloody Marys and eggs Benedict. The way the tomato juice and the spice cut the richness of the hollandaise . . . slam dunk! We prefer Sacramento Tomato Juice — it makes the best Bloody Marys in the world.

1   In a pitcher, whisk together all ingredients except the vodka, celery, and lemon.

2   Fill an 8 to 10-ounce highball glass with ice. Pour in 1½ ounces vodka and top with the tomato juice mixture. Use a celery stalk to stir and hook a slice of lemon onto the rim of the glass. Repeat with the remaining glasses.

BLUEBERRY SMASH

SERVES 2

6 fresh blueberries

6 fresh mint leaves, plus more for garnish

2 TABLESPOONS *Simple Syrup (page 210)*

Ice

2 OUNCES *dry gin*

Seltzer water

1   Divide the blueberries, mint leaves, and Simple Syrup between 2 tall glasses and muddle (bruise lightly) with the handle end of a wooden spoon.

2   Add ice to each glass.

3   Pour 1 ounce gin into each glass. Top with a splash of seltzer. Shake and serve with a mint-leaf garnish.

BELLINIS

SERVES 8

2 *white peaches*

1 TABLESPOON *confectioners' sugar*

1 TEASPOON *freshly squeezed lemon juice*

ONE 750-MILLILITER BOTTLE *champagne or sparkling wine*

....

NOTE *Make sure to taste the peaches. If they are tart or bland, you may need to add more sugar to the puree.*

1   Use a paring knife to make a shallow "X" on the underside of each peach. Place the peaches in boiling water for 15 seconds. Remove and shock in ice-cold water. Slip off the skins and remove the pits from both peaches. Coarsely chop the peaches and place them in food processor with the sugar and lemon juice. Puree the mixture.

2   Fill 8 champagne flutes one third of the way with white peach puree and top with champagne or sparkling wine.

MIMOSAS

SERVES 8

1 PINT *freshly squeezed orange juice*

ONE 750-MILLILITER BOTTLE *champagne or sparkling wine*

Fill 8 champagne flutes one third of the way with orange juice and top with champagne or sparkling wine.

· ACKNOWLEDGMENTS ·

THANKS TO . . .

OUR GUESTS: We owe much of our success to the diners, who bring great enthusiasm and appetites to our joint day after day, but we especially want to thank our regulars, who were there from the beginning, Greg Wilson, Natalie Katic, Christopher Shinn, and our mascot, Jack McKeever.

OUR SUPPLIERS: Mark Thompson of the Brooklyn Ice Cream Factory, Akiyama, Sweet Clover Farms, Bobolink Dairy, Piccinini Brothers, Blooming Hill Farm, Jeffrey's Meats, SOS Chefs, Eden Brook Fish, Ithaca Root Beer, Valente Yeast, and Basis Farm to Chef.

OUR CURRENT STAFF: We are lucky to have some of the most devoted and caring workers in New York: Chef de Cuisine Zachary Kell, Latoya Mason, Santa Diaz, Gladys Bido, Pedro Campos, Shelby Rodriguez, Cassandra Elmi, Alecia Hill, Jesse Levison, Alex Kleinberg, Trish LaRose, Evie Gaynor, Alexis Rosenbach, John Kniesly, Natalia Krasnodebska, Hugo Sanchez, Carlos Irala, Pedro Mendez, Antonio Mendez, Omar Mendez, Juan Gonzalez, Jose Perez, Ignacia Hernandez, and Andy Kopas.

OUR SOUNDING BOARD: For great ideas and sharp eyes, Emily Swanson and Dyske Suematsu. For brilliant edits and going the distance, the very clever and loyal Diane Vadino.

OUR MOONLIGHTERS: John Cheng, Caesar Balderas, and "Cousin Jay" Kurtz.

OUR SUPPORTERS: David Gordon. Also the Zabar's crew, especially Scott Goldshine.

OUR AGENTS: Renée Zuckerbrot and Martha Kaplan, for practical guidance, sage advice, and top-notch support from soup to nuts.

OUR PUBLISHER: Little, Brown and our magnanimous editor, Michael Sand, for choosing us (!) and his talented crew, including Zinzi Clemmons, designer Laura Palese, and copyeditor Jayne Yaffe Kemp, all of whom truly made our book better.

OUR PHOTOGRAPHER: Michael Harlan Turkell, for killer photos and a keen sense of food.

OUR RECIPE TESTERS: Led by the marvelous, steadfast (and heaven-sent) developer Adelaide Mueller, the following people helped us create recipes truly meant for home use. Most significantly, Susan Breslau, a tireless and valuable kitchen assistant. Additionally, the expert Anne Marie Capossela. Also Rebecca Feuer, Michelle Mahoney, Trudi "L&S" Roth, Rachel Costanza, Lisa Brickley, Aileen Monahan, Jillian Hollmann, Paula Nathanson, Debbe Gladstone, Lori Lahman, Allison Newman, Phyllis Theermann, Roxanne Wolanczyk, Karen Sonet-Rosenthal, Eileen Livers, Courtney Brietstein, Peter Lubell, Kathy Pavlica, Elyssa Koidin, Jill Koidin, Yasu Fujita, and Josh Levin.

AND LAST BUT NOT LEAST, OUR CHILDREN: Alex, Michelle, and Jade. For love, laughter, and some of the best palates known to man.

.ABOUT THE.
Authors

DeDe Lahman, co-owner of Clinton St. Baking Company and Community Food & Juice, after graduating from Simmons College began her career at *Seventeen* magazine, where she was an editor and advice columnist covering fitness, food, and relationships, from 1993 to 1998. Later, while working as a book researcher, freelance writer, and brand consultant to Coca-Cola, Inc., DeDe studied cooking and kitchen management in the New School's Culinary Arts program. She is a certified hatha yoga instructor.

Neil and DeDe first met in a chance encounter at A Salt and Battery, the takeout fish-and-chips shop in Greenwich Village. They opened Clinton St. Baking Company (www.clintonstreetbaking .com) in 2001. Together they were featured in 2004 as NY1's "New Yorker(s) of the Week."

DeDe and Neil live in Manhattan and Olive-bridge, New York, with their blended family, which includes Alex, Michelle, and Jade.

....

Neil Kleinberg is a co-owner of Clinton St. Baking Company, as well as Community Food & Juice. A culinary arts graduate of New York City College of Technology in Brooklyn, he opened his first restaurant, Simon's, in 1980 at the age of twenty-two. Simon's was the toast of Lincoln Center and the dining room for Mick Jagger, Kevin Kline, Yoko Ono, and Walter Cronkite. Since then, Neil has cooked in the kitchens of the celebrated French bistro La Colombe d'Or, the

Plaza Hotel, and the Water Club. In 1997, Neil returned to his native Flatbush, Brooklyn, to reopen the legendary seafood restaurant Lundy's, where he expedited more than a thousand sea-food dinners a night.

Neil has done live cooking demonstrations on *The Martha Stewart Show, Good Day New York, The Today Show,* and the Food Network's *Throw-down! with Bobby Flay,* among other programs. He is a recurring guest on Martha Stewart Living Radio and a distinguished member of the James Beard Foundation.

.ABOUT THE.
Photographer

Michael Harlan Turkell is a freelance photographer and the photo editor of *Edible Brooklyn* and *Edible Manhattan,* magazines that focus on local food culture. In his downtime he photographs the inner workings of kitchens for an ongoing project, "Back of the House," which documents the lives of chefs. Michael's award-winning work has appeared in an array of online publications and magazines, including *Saveur, Gastronomica, Imbibe, New York, Food & Wine,* and *Gourmet.* He lives in Brooklyn with a cat that has a beer named after him, Mason's Black Wheat by Sixpoint Craft Ale.

· INDEX ·

Page numbers in *italic* refer to photographs.